EMBROIDERY · SKILLS

CANVAS EMBROIDERY

EMBROIDERY · SKILLS

CANVAS EMBROIDERY

Peggy Field and June Linsley

DEDICATION

To all those who have inspired and helped us over the years, teachers and students, long suffering families and friends.

This edition specially produced in 1991 for
WI Books Ltd
104 New Kings Road
London SW6 4LY

By arrangement with
Merehurst Limited
Ferry House
51-57 Lacy Road
Putney
London SW15 1PR

ISBN: 1 85391 295 6

Edited by Diana Brinton
Designed by Bill Mason
Photography by Stewart Grant
(except pages 8, 118, 119)
Drawings by Peggy Field
Diagrams by Lindsay Blow
Typesetting by
Rowland Phototypesetting Limited,
Bury St Edmunds, Suffolk
Colour Separation by
Scantrans Pte Limited, Singapore
Printed in Italy by
New Interlitho SpA, Milan

CONTENTS

INTRODUCTION

The techniques of embroidery on canvas, ways to create your own designs, the range of materials that you can use, and how to use them – all these are the subject of this book, which is intended for complete beginners, for traditionalists looking for a freer approach, and for embroiderers who are experienced in other techniques but are using canvas for the first time.

The term 'canvas embroidery' has been chosen in preference to needlepoint or canvaswork, because canvas can be used in many different ways, not just for densely worked pictures or to create a hard-wearing fabric for a useful article. The guidelines and traditional procedures that have been developed over the years are outlined, but hopefully we also show that these rules do not always apply, and that some can be adapted or even dispensed with altogether. These days, embroiderers are asking themselves 'What happens if . . .?', rather than simply 'What is the correct way . . .?' and this unrestricted approach is broadening our horizons.

The simple design techniques that are demonstrated here can lead to some exciting and highly attractive embroideries, and as well as the works of established textile artists, we have included some by complete beginners. If you are a beginner, remember that when you look at old embroideries it is not always the perfectly worked piece that catches your imagination; it is often the one that reveals the personality of the maker. Sometimes this is because the embroiderer has included a personal detail, but sometimes it is due to a mistake or an obvious difficulty! Skill comes with practice.

Ray of Sunshine, *by Barbara Dawson, is an experimental panel of the 1970s in which free-stitched figures are set in a frame of formal stitchery. Threads have been frayed out from the canvas, wrapped and applied as rays of sunshine.*

From past to present

Needlepoint as we know it today started in the sixteenth century, when the new middle class, anxious to add touches of luxury to their homes, began to make embroideries in imitation of the huge woven tapestries that adorned the houses of the aristocracy. The resulting confusion between *woven* tapestries and *embroidered* needlepoint (or canvaswork) has lasted to this day.

Over the centuries, needlepoint fashions changed. In Elizabethan times, the many cushions, covers and hangings were decorated with realistic garden flowers and devices with allegorical meanings; the 17th century saw a fashion for small Biblical pictures and minor decorative items, the flowers becoming more exotic as the century progressed. In the 18th century, small naturalistic flowers and leaves

Above *A design chart for Berlin woolwork of the 1860s.*

Left The Discovery of the Infant Moses by the Nile *is an English pictorial panel or cushion cover of the mid-17th century. The embroidery is of silk, tent-stitched on a linen ground, the faces being left unstitched. The motifs were taken from contemporary pattern books published by Peter Stent and John Overton (see Johnstone 1986). Embroiderer's Guild Collection E.G.5860.*

decorated sets of upholstered chairs, carpets and screens, and tent stitch continued in popularity.

In the Victorian era, there was a craze for cross-stitch patterns, worked in chemically dyed Berlin wools. The patterns were often taken from magazines and the results sometimes appear crude and garish to modern eyes, but to the Victorians the new dyes must have seemed as exciting as metallic threads are to us today.

This century has seen a new, more experimental attitude to needlepoint. Creative embroiderers are combining it with other techniques, and they question the need to cover the entire background or to work with wool alone. Paints and dyes are used, and the qualities of bare, unstitched canvas are exploited. There is at least as much scope for experimentation in this ancient technique as in any other textile craft, and there are clues throughout its history, waiting to be seized upon and developed in a thoroughly modern way.

CHAPTER 1

MATERIALS AND BASIC TECHNIQUES

Canvas

Needlepoint embroidery is carried out on a fairly stiff, open, even-weave fabric, made of cotton or linen and usually white, cream or beige in colour. Its degree of fineness is described by the number of threads or holes to each 2.5cm (1in.), and grades range from very fine, with over 30 threads to each 2.5cm (1in.), to a large open-mesh rug canvas with 5 or 7 threads. There are two main weaves – single and double – described below.

A beginner might choose a single canvas with 12 or 14 threads per 2.5cm (1in.). It should preferably be white or cream so that dye may be applied if desired. Most craft shops and department stores will stock canvases of this type, and although prices may seem to vary enormously they take into account the width, composition and country of origin of the different canvases. To begin with, the cheapest quality will do, but there is great pleasure in working on smoother, polished, 'de luxe' quality.

About 25 to 30cm (10 to 12in.), whatever the width, will be enough for a try-out piece, a sampler of some kind and a small finished piece. Always allow for a good margin of unworked canvas all around your design: 5cm (2in.) is the absolute minimum, more is necessary for larger items.

Single canvas

Also known as mono canvas, this has single threads interwoven vertically and horizontally. A 12s mono label indicates a fairly coarse canvas – a single weave with 12 threads per 2.5cm (1in.). Some canvases have a twisted warp thread, but the count is the same.

Double or Penelope canvas

Here, the interwoven threads are grouped in pairs. This canvas is usually described by the number of holes between the double

Some of the many different kinds of canvas available today: the pansies have been worked from the same chart, each with the same number of stitches, on canvases ranging from 22s to 10s. Some canvas has been coloured.

threads, though sometimes the threads are counted as well. A Penelope 16/32 will therefore be a medium double canvas, with 32 threads – in pairs – to each 2.5cm (1in.), providing 16 holes.

The double threads make it easier to count when cross stitches are being worked, but this canvas is less versatile than single, as you cannot use it for vertical or horizontal stitches. For areas of fine work in a panel – faces, hands, minute details – the double threads may be prised apart, making a fine single mesh. Called 'pricking the ground', this is often seen in Victorian needlepoint.

Rug canvas

This is a coarse canvas with 3, 5, or 7 holes to each 2.5cm (1in.). It is usually cream in colour and is often marked out in a grid of ten holes, shown by a brown thread. A plastic version is available, and in America most rug canvas is washable.

Plastic canvas

A relatively new medium, this has a fairly coarse mesh, which is generally of translucent plastic, though pastel colours are available from specialist suppliers. It is semi-rigid and can be cut to shape easily without fraying. Plastic canvas is usually bought in sheets measuring either 37cm × 27cm (13½in. × 10½in.) or 45cm × 30cm (17½in. × 12in.). Pre-formed circles, ovals and other shapes are available for items such as box lids.

Perforated paper

Originally used for Victorian card-work, this has 14 holes per 2.5cm (1in.). It comes in sheets measuring 31cm × 23cm (12in. × 9in.) and is quite strong. It may be rolled, in one direction only, without weakening it significantly.

Evenweave fabrics

Any kind of evenweave fabric, such as linen, may be used. Such fabrics are more suitable for wearable items because of their flexibility. Other fabrics with a square mesh may be useful for experimental pieces.

Threads

In past times, the criterion for choosing a thread was whether it covered the canvas sufficiently well to produce an even, hard-wearing fabric. This may be what you need, in which case you will require purpose-made threads – tapestry wools, either plied or stranded; Persian wools, which have three separate strands loosely twisted together, or fine crewel wools, also with three strands, but more firmly twisted. Rich silk threads may also be used.

These are available in a wide range of subtly graded colours, but

they are expensive. If you are a beginner, or wish to expand your skills, a more adventurous and economical course is to assemble threads you already have. Anything that will go through the eye of a needle may come in useful – oddments of fancy knitting wool, crochet yarn, stranded embroidery cotton, sewing machine threads, metallic threads, fine string, plastic string, garden twine, fine ribbons, even fabric cut into thin strips. Group them into categories – mat, shiny, fine and thick, and textured and smooth. If you have to go out and buy threads, restrict yourself to shades of one colour, with perhaps one contrast, and again find a good range.

In decorative work the thread need not cover the canvas completely. Two different threads may be used together in the needle, and textured or bouclé threads may be coaxed through the canvas or couched down on top.

Sun on Mud Flats, *by Elise Warren, is embroidered in tent stitch. A wide range of unusual threads has been used to convey the effect of brilliant sunlight on darker mud flat areas.*

Precise amounts of wool are not needed for the ideas in this book. However, if you intend to work a large area in one stitch and in one background colour, the best way, though this may be laborious, is to work a 2.5cm (1in.) square with measured lengths of wool. Work out approximately the area covered by this colour in your design, and multiply the two figures. For a more interesting solid background, you can use two strands in the needle at a time, mixing shades of the background colour: this makes precise calculation unnecessary.

Tapestry needles

A tapestry needle has a large eye that can easily be threaded and a blunt point, so that it will not split either the threads of the canvas itself or the embroidery thread, when stitches share the same hole. When threaded, the needle should pass easily through the canvas without pushing the mesh threads out of place. Sizes range from size 13 for very coarse work to 24 or 26 for fine work. A size 18 or 20 is perhaps the best for general purposes; a pack of assorted sizes is also useful.

A tapestry needle is ideal for needlepoint, but if you are tempted to use the sharp pointed version – a chenille needle – turn it round and pass the eye end through the canvas.

Frames

It is best to work on a frame from the start. The embroidery will remain flat, taut and in shape, both while you are working and when it is put away. Even more importantly, the stitches will be formed correctly, each with two movements of the needle, down through the canvas with one movement and then up from the back as a second movement. With practice, one hand can remain on the top of the work, the other below, maintaining an even tension and keeping diagonal distortion of the canvas to a minimum.

Simple frames (1, 2)

A square or rectangular frame is essential; a ring frame will distort the mesh of the canvas as it is stretched over the lower ring. For most small projects, any of the following may be used:

Preparing a simple frame

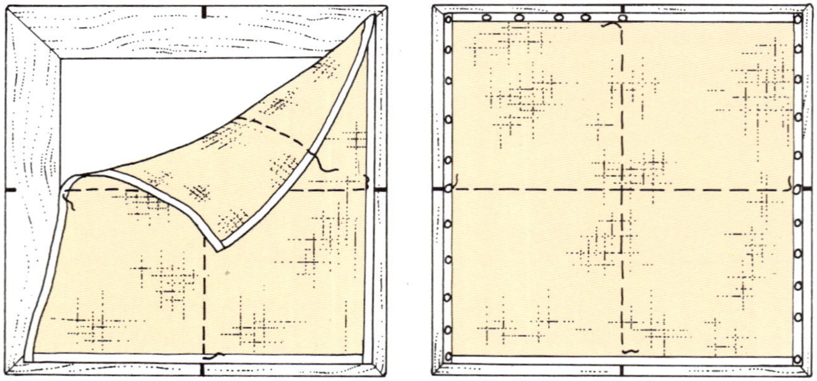

1 **Mark the centre of each side of the frame. Cut the canvas very slightly smaller than the outer measurement of the frame and cover the edges with masking tape. Mark the centre of the canvas by basting right across, both ways.**

2 **Match the centre points of the canvas and frame, top and bottom. Starting from the top centre and working outwards to one side then the other, secure with drawing pins (thumb tacks) through the masking tape, at intervals of about 12mm (½in.). Repeat at the bottom, keeping the canvas taut and straight. Turn the frame and repeat the process so that the sides are secured in the same way.**

- the back of an old picture frame
- two pairs of artists' stretchers (these have corners already mitred and slotted ready to be assembled)
- a home-made frame with four pieces of 12mm × 20mm (½in. × ¾in.) wood, joined with a simple mitred joint or with a flat L-bracket. A good size for this fairly rudimentary type of frame would be about 30cm × 20cm (12in. × 8in.). The canvas is attached with drawing pins (thumb tacks) or staples.

Embroidery frames (3, 4, 5)

For a heavily stitched, large-scale piece, use a commercially-made adjustable frame. This consists of two horizontal rollers with webbing attached and two side slats, put together with screws or pegs. The canvas must be fixed 'square' onto it so that the pull is even. The edges of the canvas must be protected from fraying with tape.

Dressing a roller frame

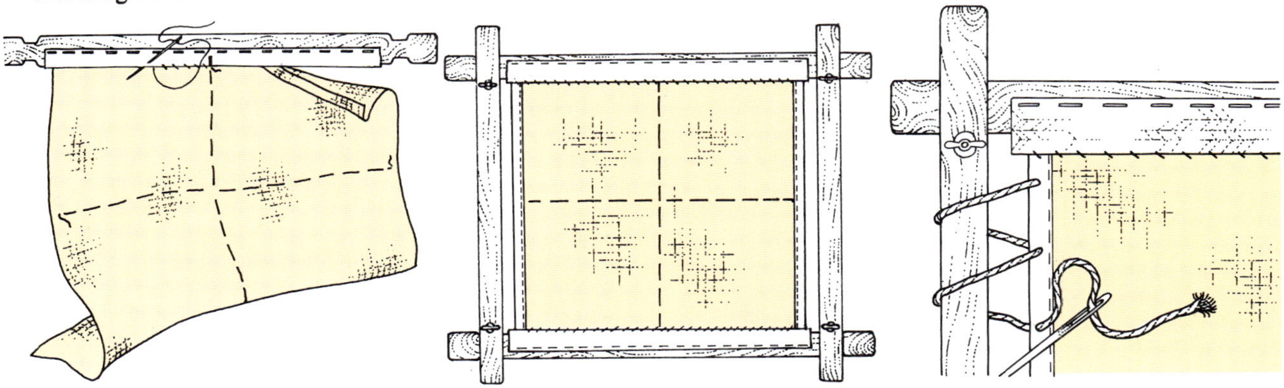

3 **Turn under four threads of canvas at the top and bottom, and mark the centres as before with lines of basting stitches. With the frame dismantled, match top centres of canvas and webbing, and stitch the canvas to the webbing, starting from the top centre and working outwards. Repeat at the bottom edge.**

4 **Baste strong binding tape along the side edges of the canvas. Fit the rollers, with canvas attached, into the side struts, rolling up any surplus canvas. Secure by the pegs or screws provided, and adjust until the canvas is taut.**

5 **With strong thread, lace the sides of the canvas over the sides of the frame, making stitches about 2.5cm (1in.) apart. This will support the canvas sides, but will have to be undone and resewn if the surplus canvas is unrolled for subsequent working.**

Enlarging a design (1)

Squaring up is a simple yet effective way of enlarging – or reducing – a design. The method shown here, in which the original is copied, square for square, onto a grid, takes time, but avoids accidental distortion. (Deliberate distortions, incidentally, in which the design is copied onto a grid with the same number of divisions, but different proportions, can produce interesting designs.) Books of tracing graph paper are available, and these are a useful time-saver.

Commercial photocopying agencies will also enlarge or reduce designs, though this may be expensive.

If you have a transparency of a drawing or design, you can use a slide projector to scale it up. Project the image onto a piece of white paper or tracing paper, fixed to the wall. By moving the projector forward and back you can see the design in different sizes, and decide which will suit your purpose. When you have chosen, draw the projected image on the paper.

1 **Draw a frame around the design. Place tracing paper over it and trace the frame. Extend a diagonal line out from the bottom left corner, through the top right corner, to the required height, and complete the larger frame.**

Draw a grid, with the same number of squares over each frame. Transfer the design, square by square, to the second frame. The same process can be used, this time making the second frame smaller, to reduce the size of a design.

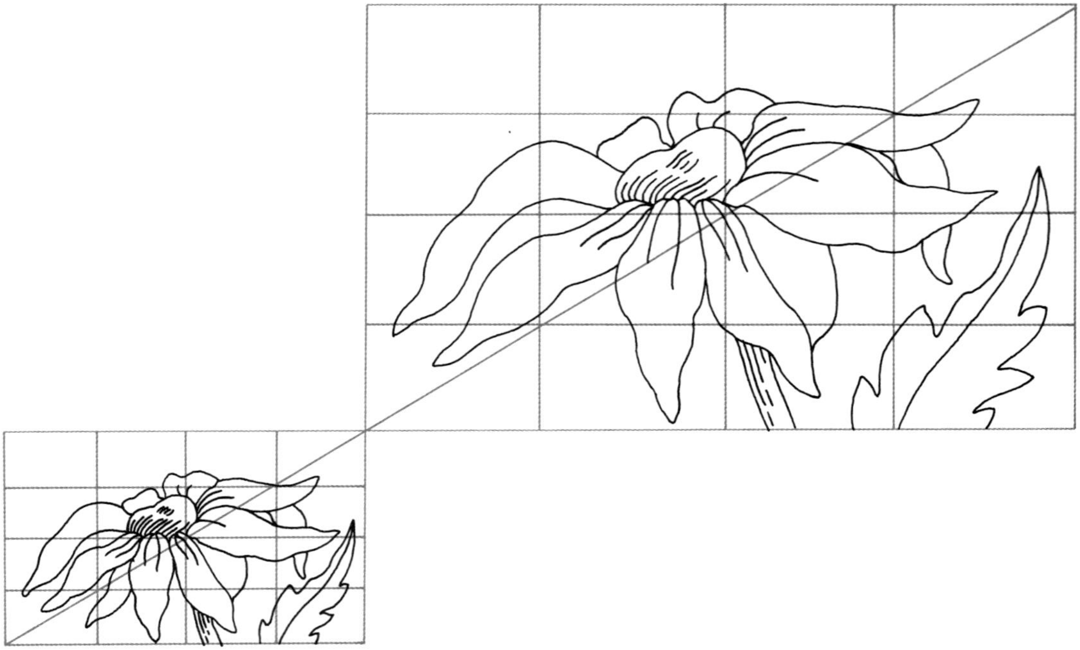

Transferring a design to canvas (2, 3)

A well-tried method of transferring a design to canvas is to trace the design on graph paper, using the grid to make your outline geometric, and then colouring in your own chart. If your graph paper corresponds with the size of the canvas, so much the better, otherwise small test pieces can be worked. Work your stitches, counting from the chart and remembering that each square on the graph paper represents one thread. This method is best for designs using tent and cross stitches.

It is possible to draw a very black outline round your design on paper. This will show through most grades of canvas so that you can trace the design directly onto the canvas: a word of warning, however – a waterproof pen or coloured pencil must be used. Should the finished piece need damp stretching, a non-permanent marker would run, ruining your precious embroidery. A water-soluble quilters' pen may be used, as this outline will disappear when wet.

A full design may be painted on canvas, either freely or by filling in a traced outline. Again, care should be taken to use paint that will not affect the thread: oil paints can be used but they may be sticky; acrylic paints are preferable. Acrylic paints can be sponged away before they are completely dry, but once dry, mistakes become permanent because the paints form a plastic skin. Fabric paints need not be fixed with heat if they are used merely to indicate the design, rather than to decorate an unworked background.

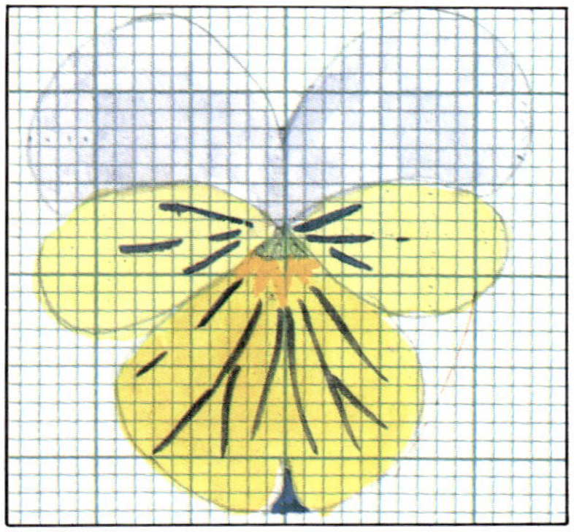

2 **A design may be worked out on graph paper, each square representing one intersection of canvas threads. For a large design, it may be useful to mark horizontal and vertical guidelines, at ten-thread intervals.**

3 **Run over the design outlines a second time, using a felt tip pen. Use a waterproof pen or coloured pencil when tracing the design directly on canvas. If you cannot see the outlines through the canvas, tape the design and then the canvas to a window.**

Damp stretching (1, 2)

If your finished work is not quite straight, it may be necessary to block (damp stretch) it before mounting or making up. In any case, damp stretching will improve the general appearance of the embroidery, just as pressing improves knitting or dress-making.

The dampness loosens the stiffening element in the canvas, which is stretched, pinned into shape, and allowed to dry naturally. There are several different ways of doing this, but the following works very well. You will need a piece of thick wooden board, larger than the embroidery, and soft enough to take drawing pins or tacks; four or five sheets of newspaper or blotting paper; a top sheet of plain white paper, with the outline of your embroidery drawn out with waterproof marker, and drawing pins (brass, if possible, to avoid rust). If the piece is badly distorted, you can repeat the process.

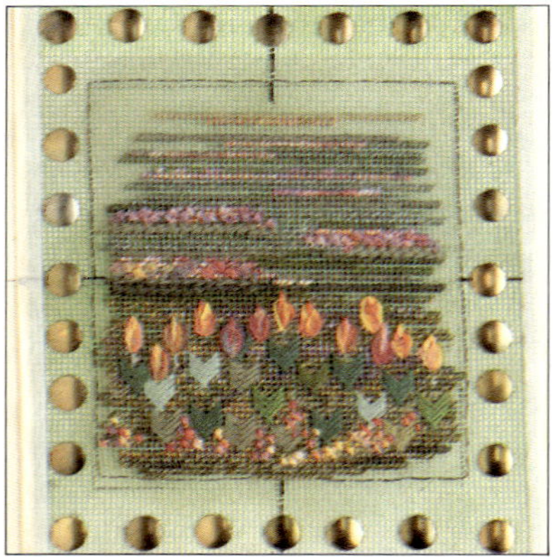

1 Place layers of paper on a board and wet them thoroughly. On top, lay a sheet of white paper with the outline of your finished piece of embroidery marked on it with a waterproof pen or a pencil. The centre lines should also be drawn on the paper, and centre points marked on each side of the embroidery.

2 Lay the embroidery right side up on the paper, matching the centre points. Starting from the top centre and working outwards, insert drawing pins (thumb tacks) outside the embroidered area at intervals of about 2.5cm (1in.), closer if the work is very distorted. Pull the canvas straight, and pin along bottom edge to match drawn shape.

Match, pull and pin the sides in the same way, and then leave the canvas to dry naturally. This may take two to three days. If the canvas is still not quite square when unpinned, repeat the whole process.

Lacing and mounting (3, 4)

If you are framing a finished embroidery, you will probably need to lace it over hardboard to keep it flat and in shape. If you are using a card window surround or presenting the piece as a greetings card, you may simply staple the embroidery to board or card. The staples will be hidden, though they will eventually rust through.

For lacing, there should be a margin of unworked canvas of at least 5cm (2in.), more for larger pieces, to allow for the pull of the lacing, but if you have worked too near the edge you can extend the area with fabric strips: they will not be seen. The hardboard should fit loosely in the frame, allowing for the canvas turnings. Mark the centres of the sides to line up with the centre marks on the canvas.

You will need a piece of hardboard, drawing pins (thumb tacks), a sharp needle and strong thread.

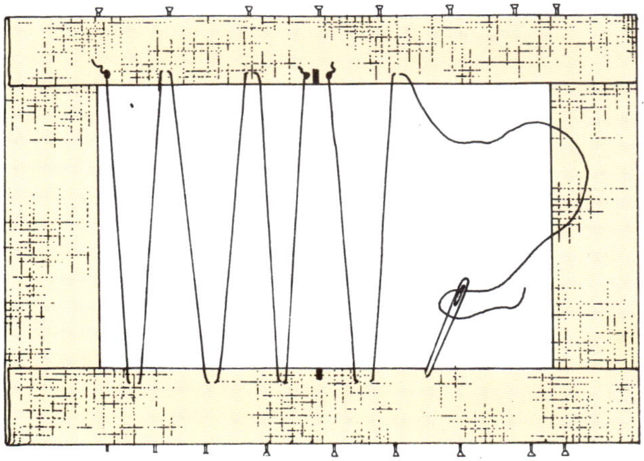

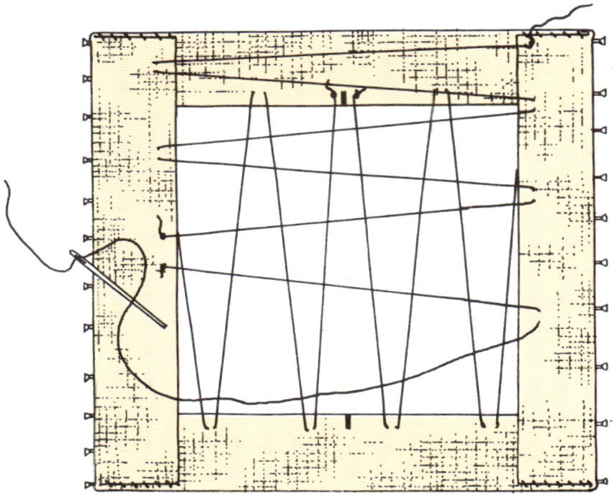

3 Lay the embroidery on top of the board, matching centre points. Fold the top and bottom allowances to the back, securing them temporarily with pins. Fasten a long thread securely at the centre top. Lace from top to bottom, working first to the left. Take up several threads of the canvas with each stitch to prevent them pulling away. Fasten off temporarily, leaving a tail of thread. Return to the centre and with a new piece of thread work out to the right.

4 When this lacing is complete, remove the pins. Return to the centre and pull each stitch tighter, taking up any slack. At each end, fasten the lacing thread securely. A dab of glue may prevent any slackening. The sides are laced in the same way.

The corners of the canvas may be mitred, but it is sufficient to fold over the edges and secure them with a few stitches. When lacing is complete, a piece of thick paper may be glued in place, to cover the back.

Seams

If your embroidery is to be used for a practical purpose, you must consider from the outset whether seams will be required. Canvas seams can be very bulky, building up into multiple layers of canvas that are very difficult to handle.

One solution is to use plastic canvas, cutting the sections to the finished size and then whipstitching them together. If you have chosen a flexible canvas, you might consider using a matching fabric backing instead of joining two layers of canvas. This would give a pleasant change of texture as well as reducing the bulkiness of the seams. A firm woollen fabric, corduroy or velvet would be suitable.

Plan the construction of the article carefully, with special reference to the seams. For example, if you are making a case for glasses, the usual construction is a long strip, folded in the centre and doubled back. If, however, you make a flattened cylinder, you will only need to join one long seam and the short bottom seam, and the case will be much stronger. Larger articles, such as cushions and bags, are often easier to make up, as the greater area of worked canvas is easier to manoeuvre, allowing seams to be machined or backstitched.

Preparation

In general, success with seams depends on forward planning, careful matching of canvas threads, and basting the canvas before making any embroidery stitches.

Damp stretch the embroidery, if necessary, then trim away excess unworked canvas, leaving about 1.5cm (5/8in.) for small articles and up to 5cm (2in.) for larger ones. If the canvas is very loosely woven, put small dabs of glue at intersections where threads may fray.

A whipped seam (1, 2, 3)

When stitched as shown here, this makes an almost invisible seam. For a strong, braided effect, leave two threads uncovered at each edge and cover the join with long-legged cross stitch.

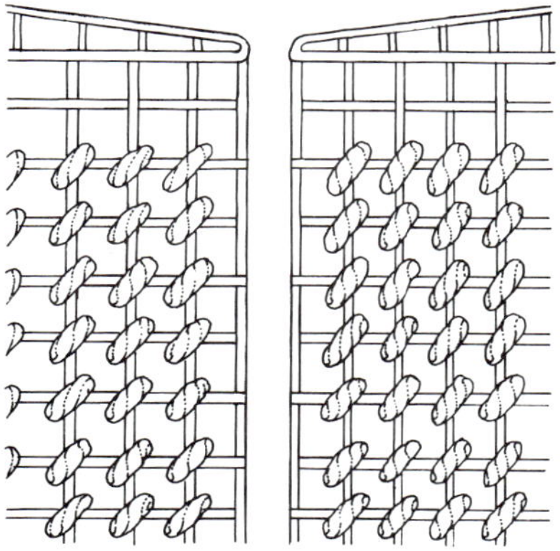

1 On each piece to be joined, fold the spare canvas to the back of the work, leaving one unworked thread visible on the top.

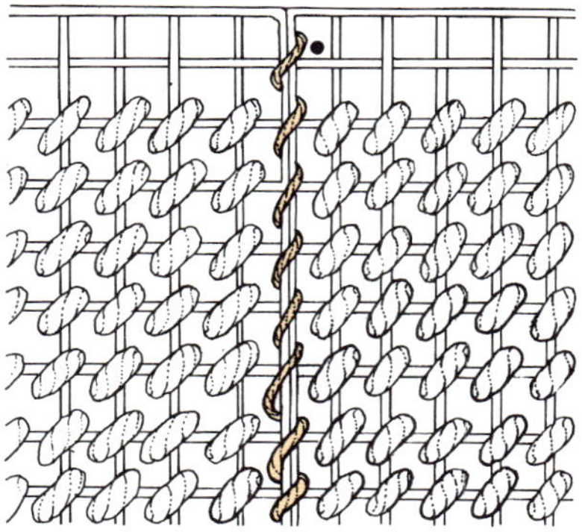

2 With right sides of the work facing you, carefully match up the threads of the edges to be joined. Use a strong fine neutral-coloured thread to whip the edges together, starting from the top.

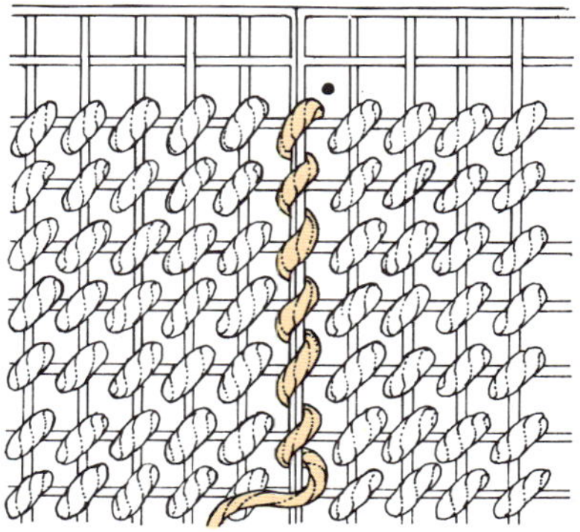

3 Work a row of tent stitch or half cross stitch over the join, using a contrasting or matching wool, as you require. Blindstitch the unworked seam allowances to the back of the stitched canvas.

An overlapped seam

Leave from 1 to 2cm (½ to ¾in.) of unworked canvas, depending on the size of the canvas mesh, along each edge to be joined. With right sides up, lay one unworked edge over the other and baste them together, matching the canvas threads exactly. Make the final embroidery stitches through both thicknesses of canvas, covering the cut edge of the overlapping canvas.

Seaming canvas to fabric

With right sides together, lay the trimmed canvas on matching fabric, cut to the same size. With the canvas uppermost, backstitch or machine the seam, stitching along the last row of holes of the embroidery.

CHAPTER 2

STITCHES AND THEIR USES

This is not a complete stitch dictionary, but a selection of favourite and useful stitches that may be used either formally or experimentally. Needlepoint stitches are not just a way of filling specific areas: they have a beauty of their own when used individually, and once you begin to experiment with them, in the same way that you might experiment with surface stitches, you will discover your own exciting and interesting variations.

Instead of showing the stitches one by one, grouped into categories such as cross stitches or diagonal stitches, we have included possible experiments and variations throughout this section, with the aim of encouraging experimentation with the stitches as you practise them. First, learn and understand the stitch. If possible, try some of the variations illustrated. These may involve an unusual choice of thread, a change of colour within the stitch, a variation of scale, or completing only part of the stitch. Look for variations of your own, and when you have made a stitch, ask yourself: 'What does this stitch look like? What can I use it for?' This is one of the best ways to begin making your own designs.

Many books state that certain stitches are worked from left to right and others from right to left. In some cases, there is a reason: it may be easier to learn a stitch this way; it may be more economical in time and materials, or it may provide a thicker backing for the stitch. In other cases; the direction of stitching may not matter. Bearing these possibilities in mind, look for the way of working that suits you best.

A try-out sampler showing variations of rice stitch, Rhodes stitch, eyelets, leaf and velvet stitch. Experiments include changing the colour and the kind of thread within the stitch, varying the size and working only part of the stitch.

Using the diagrams

The needle is not shown in the stitch diagrams, as this may suggest that the stitch is scooped up. Instead, follow the numbers on the diagrams, bringing the needle up through the canvas at 1, down at 2, and following through the remaining numbers.

Count the threads of the canvas, not the holes. A 'thread' is one vertical or horizontal canvas thread; an 'intersection' is a crossing of a vertical and a horizontal thread. A square may therefore be described as either 'over four horizontal threads and four verticals' or 'over four intersections' (diagonally).

Starting and finishing

Begin by taking a tapestry needle and threading it with thread that suits the mesh of your canvas, filling the hole without packing it too densely. The thread should not be too long – from index finger to elbow is a good enough guide – we all hate threading needles, but long lengths will roughen as they pass repeatedly through the canvas. Cut the thread from the skein; if you break it, the wool will stretch and become uneven. If a thicker thread is needed, take two lengths: do not thread the needle with single length and double it back, or the wool fibres will lie in different directions.

Start and finish by running from 3 to 5cm (between 1 and 2in.) of thread through the back of existing stitches, or sew the end in as you go. Do not make knots on the back of the work.

It is not worth attempting a sampler at this point: to be successful, a sampler needs a degree of planning. Instead, keep a piece of canvas as a try-out piece, making it as neat or untidy as you please.

UPRIGHT GOBELIN

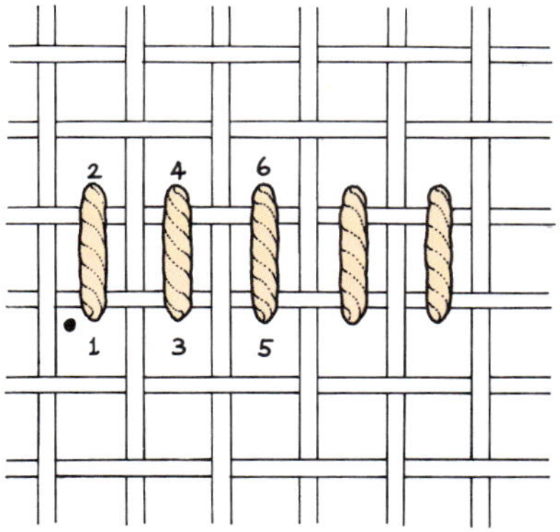

Also known as straight Gobelin, upright Gobelin is a vertical stitch, usually over two threads. It may be worked over a tramming stitch to give a padded effect and to make the finished piece more hard wearing. The threads of the canvas may be seen between the rows.

Slanting Gobelin is the same as upright Gobelin, but the stitches slant to the right over one thread of canvas.

ENCROACHING GOBELIN

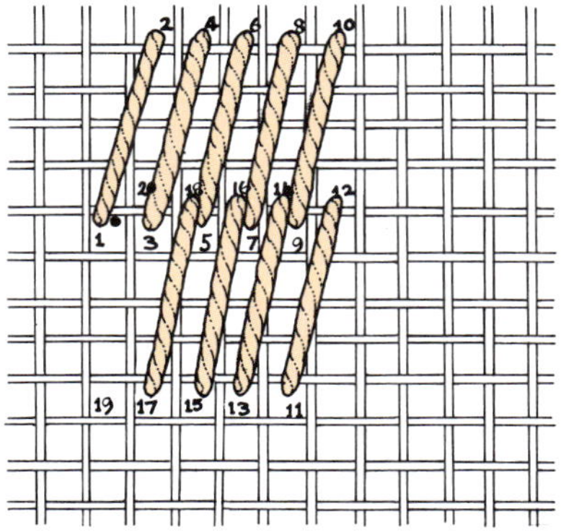

A useful stitch for shading, this has longer stitches than slanting Gobelin. Each stitch runs over five horizontal threads and diagonally over one thread. Each row overlaps the preceding row by one horizontal thread.

FILLING GOBELIN

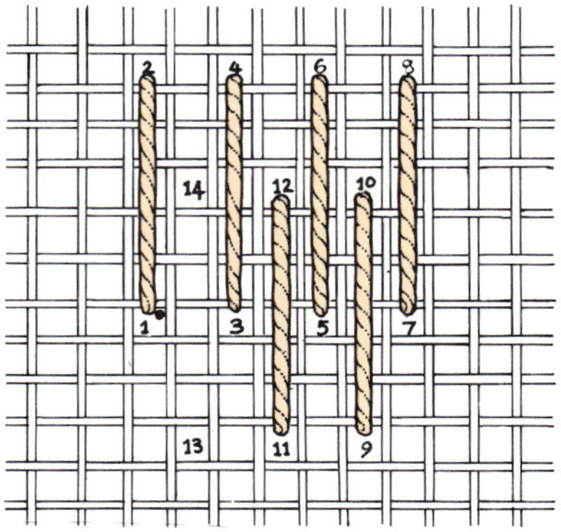

Long upright stitches are worked over six threads, leaving two threads between each stitch. The second row is spaced three threads below the first, the stitches fitting neatly into the empty spaces. Half stitches may be used to straighten the top and bottom rows.

RICE STITCH

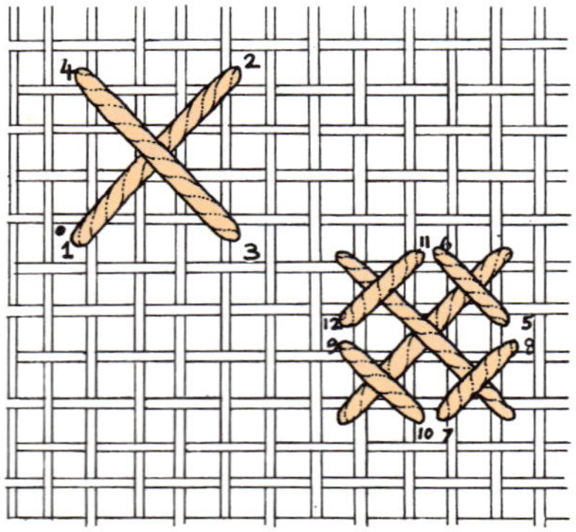

Also known as crossed corners and as William and Mary stitch, rice stitch is a large cross stitch, worked over a square of two or four threads, with a smaller diagonal back stitch crossing each arm. This is sometimes worked with a finer thread. The small stitches may be worked in any convenient order.

If you are covering a large area, you may stitch all the larger crosses first and then the smaller stitches, making one or more journeys.

SIMPLIFIED RICE STITCH

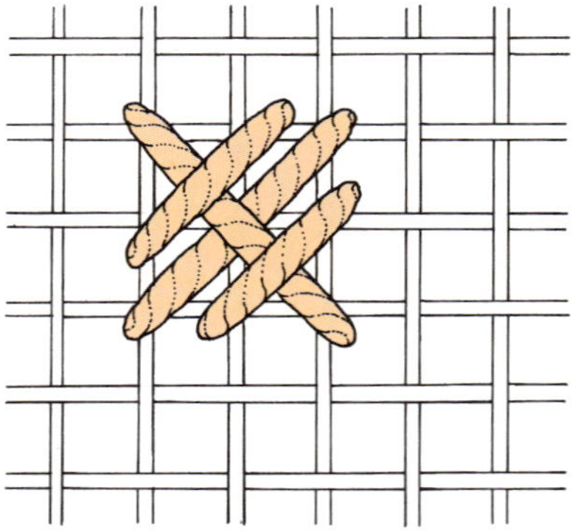

This is worked over three threads, with only two small diagonal stitches across the arms of the cross stitch. Some of the many possible variations may be seen on the class sampler.

RHODES STITCH

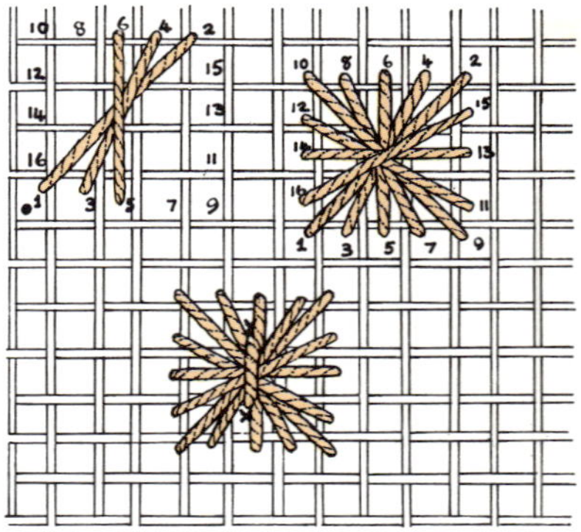

This is a raised square stitch, worked over a square of four, six or eight threads. Start with a long diagonal over four (six, eight) intersections of the canvas and work around the square, as shown in the numbered diagram. A small vertical stitch may be added when these eight (12, 16) stitches have been completed: ease the needle through the existing stitches to hold the centre threads at X and Y.

This try-out class sampler by May Beason, Yvonne Hines and Frances Wells shows experiments with simplified rice stitch. Variations come from changes of colour within the stitch and from working a mirror image of the stitch, but the size and basic elements of the stitch remain the same.

TENT STITCH

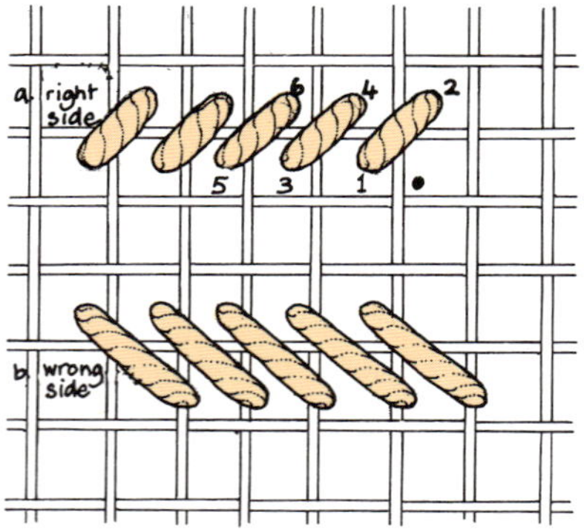

This looks like half cross, but the wrong side reveals a long slanting stitch. The stitch uses more thread than half cross, but extra padding makes the work more hard wearing.

When you have finished one row, working from right to left, turn the work upside down and work the next row, checking that you are making long slanting stitches on the wrong side, not small verticals. Stitch any motif first, then fill in the background.

DIAGONAL TENT STITCH

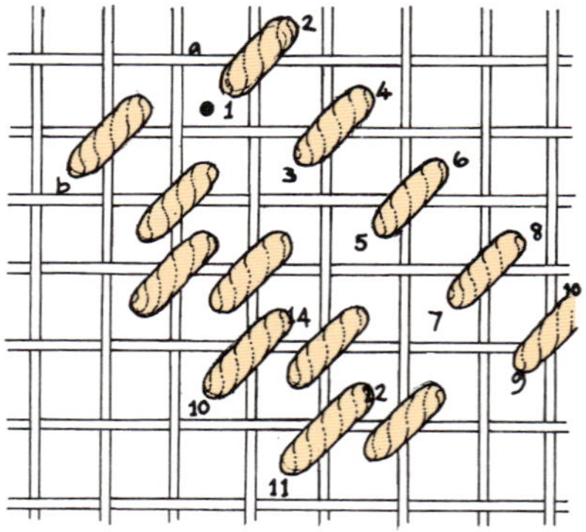

Also known as basketweave, because of the appearance of the back of the work, this way of working tent stitch causes less distortion of the canvas than the previous version. Begin at the top left of the area to be filled and stitch down to the bottom right. The second row begins at the bottom, to the left of the first row. The small area on the lower left side of the picture shows the reverse of the stitch.

HALF CROSS STITCH

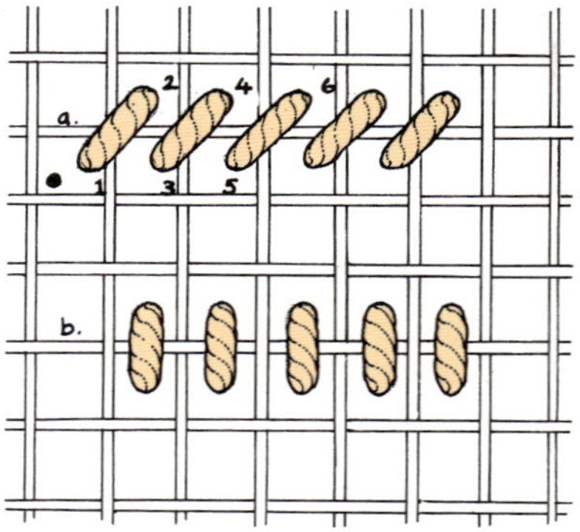

A small diagonal stitch, taken over one or two intersections of the canvas, half cross, when made with a thick thread, looks like tent stitch but is not as hard wearing. The difference is only obvious at the back, as shown here. Make sure that all the stitches in each row slant in the same direction.

STAR STITCH

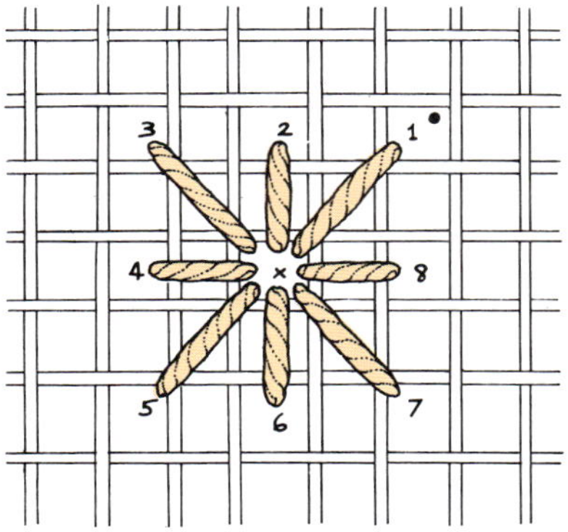

Also known as Algerian stitch, star stitch is a group of eight stitches, all worked into a central hole and arranged to cover a square of four or any even number of threads. The stitches may be pulled slightly to emphasize the central hole. (If each stitch is worked twice into the same hole before passing on to the next, the result is called Algerian eye stitch.) If the canvas is not covered completely, a lacy effect is obtained. Bring the thread up at 1, down at X, up at 2, down at X and so on.

SQUARE EYE STITCH

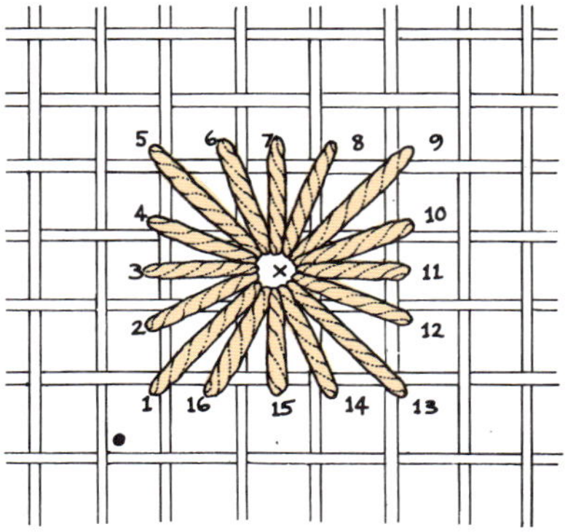

Also known as eyelet stitch, this is similar to star stitch, but more densely packed. Based on a square of four threads each way, a stitch is worked into the centre from every hole around the edge of the square – 16 altogether. The stitch may also cover a rectangle, and the central hole may be moved off centre to create an asymmetric effect.

Bring the thread up at 1, down at X, up at 2, down at X, and so on.

DIAMOND EYELET

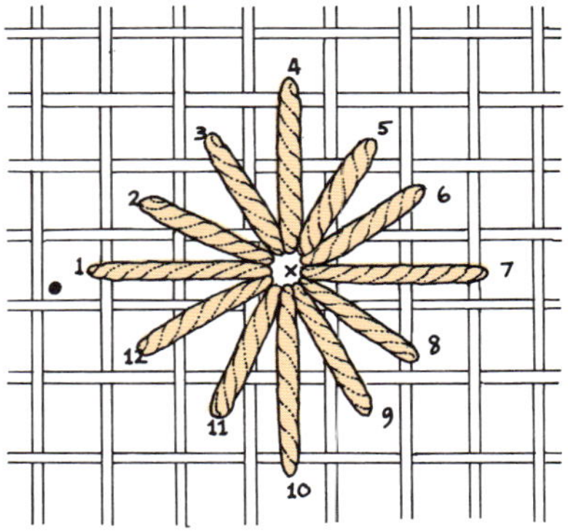

Eyelet stitches are here worked in a diamond shape, covering six threads altogether, vertically and horizontally. Follow the diagram, working each stitch into the central hole at X. Count carefully when making diamond eyelet, because some of the stitches must be shorter than others, to create the correct diamond shape. (The stitches on this page are all best worked in soft wool, as many threads must pass through the central hole.)

Making a Decorative Square

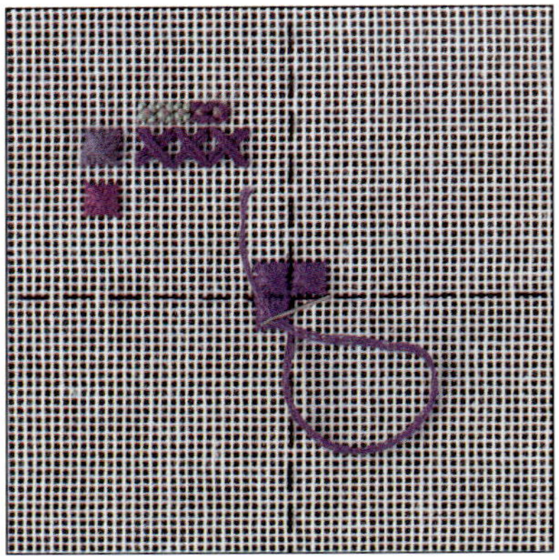

1 It is easy to make decorative squares, using a limited number of stitches. Choose a variety of threads – light and dark, mat and shiny – to be combined in a particular colour scheme. In the centre of your canvas, marked by tacking, work four Rhodes stitches, each over four threads. They will share the same holes on the centre lines. This group will occupy a square of eight threads each way. You can use the edge of the canvas to try out stitches and threads.

2 Next make two rows of half cross or tent stitch around the square, making sure that all the stitches slope in the same direction. The square will now occupy 12 threads each way. (If you work only one row, the square will be of 10 threads, which will make it difficult to fit in the stitches of the next round.)

3 A round of rice stitch comes next. If you make each stitch over four threads, this will cover the ground quickly; alternatively, the stitches may be worked over two threads for a finer effect. Stitch all the large crosses first, then fill in all the smaller diagonal stitches.

4 Add further rounds until you have reached a suitable size. Trim away the surplus canvas, leaving an allowance of about 1.5cm (½in.). Mount the sample as a small panel or greetings card, or back it with a matching fabric and make it into a small cushion or pincushion.

First attempts at canvas embroidery by Rosemary Marshall, Brenda Tubbs and Beryl Wright.

FERN STITCH

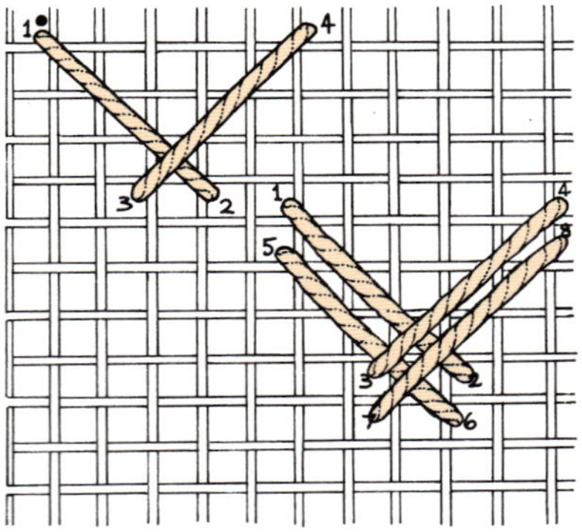

A useful stitch for foliage or for feathers, fern stitch is worked from the top down, over an even number of vertical threads (the width), the central two forming a centre vein or plait. It may be much wider or narrower than the diagram. Bring the needle up at 1, then count four threads down and four across to find 2. Bring the needle up again two threads to the left at 3, and down again at 4, making a large, top-heavy cross stitch. Stitch downward for the required length. The stitch may also run horizontally.

LEAF STITCH

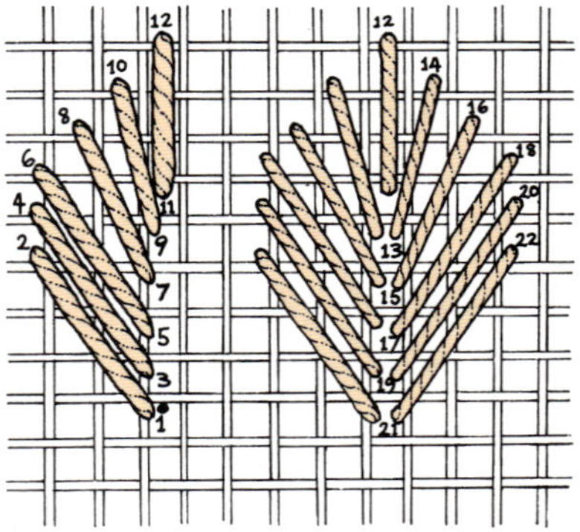

Count from the central vein of the leaf. This version is six threads wide (three each way from the centre), so begin at the lower centre and complete the first half of the leaf. The second half mirrors the first, sharing the same holes of the centre vein. If this is used as a filling stitch, the second leaf will begin six threads to the right of the vein of the first. The second row begins six threads below and three threads right of the vein of the first leaf of the first row.

VELVET STITCH

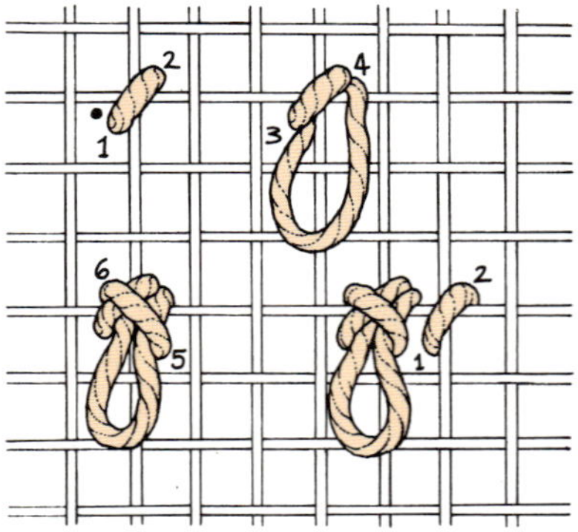

This raised pile stitch may be left in loops or clipped to make a thick velvety effect. Make stitch 1–2, the first half of a cross stitch, then make loop 3–4 through the same holes. Complete the cross stitch to hold the loop in place.

When even loops are required, they may be worked over a pencil or strip of card. Begin at the bottom when covering a large area, so that the loops do not get in your way as you stitch. Fill the whole area before clipping any loops.

Jane Trowbridge and Shirley Staniforth were new to needlepoint when they stitched these small garden panels. Groups of flowers are reduced to simple shapes formed with a limited number of needlepoint stitches. Darning and Cretan stitches are used in the background to contrast with the formal stitches.

CUSHION STITCH

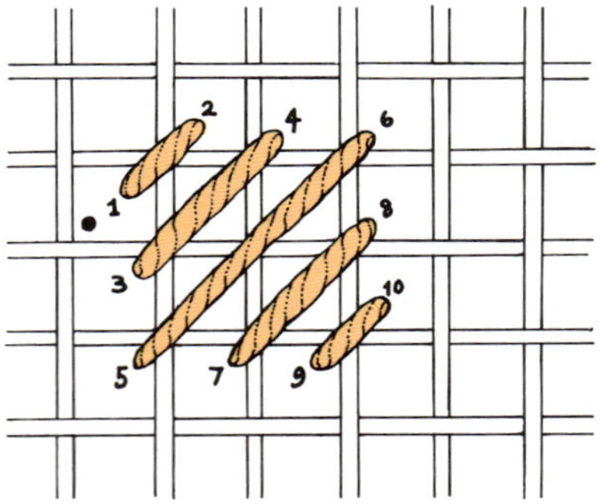

Also known as flat stitch or diagonal satin stitch, this is a group of small diagonal satin stitches, forming a small square over three or four threads. The squares may be repeated exactly or mirror imaged. Interesting effects can be obtained by changing colour halfway through the stitch.

CHEQUER STITCH

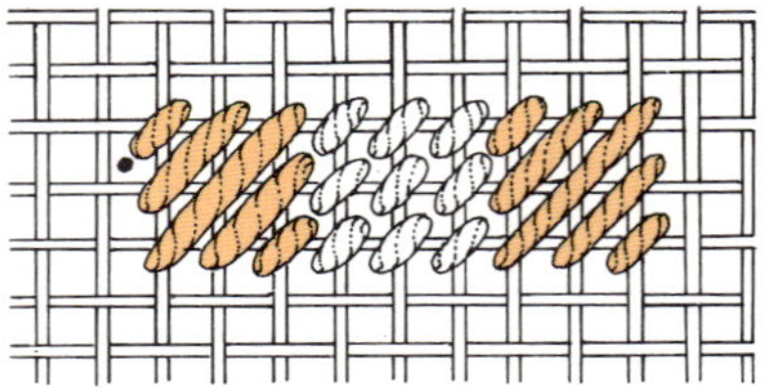

For this pattern/stitch, small cushion stitch squares are alternated with squares of tent stitch.

SCOTTISH STITCH

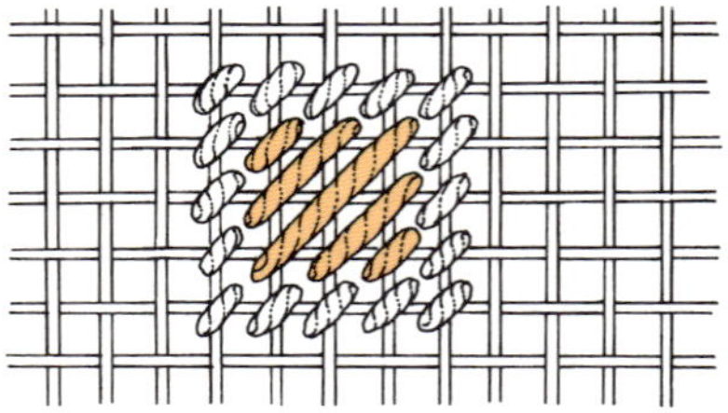

In this variation, each cushion stitch square is surrounded by a line of tent stitches.

DIAGONAL STITCH

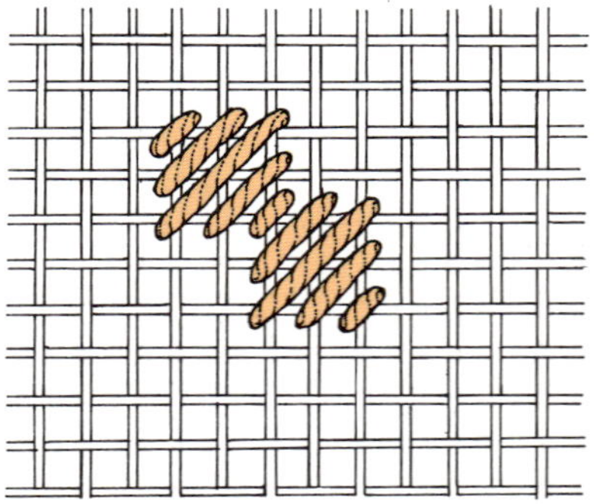

Here, the cushion stitch pattern is extended into long diagonal bands. The small diagonal stitch completing the square is counted as the first stitch of the second square. In the second row, the longest stitch fits into the same hole as the shortest stitch of the previous row.

NORWICH STITCH

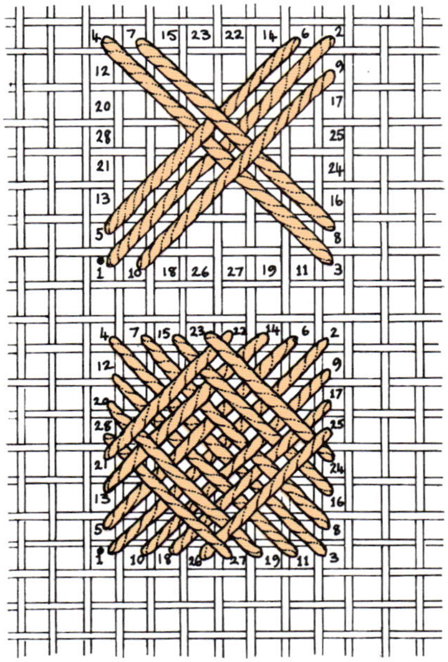

This is worked over a square of any uneven number of threads, and is most effective when a tightly spun thread is used. It is not as difficult as it looks, because the stitches follow a regular pattern. The last stitch (27–28) passes under stitch 21–22 before going into the canvas at 28 to complete the interweaving.

In Shades of Alsace, *by Frances Wells, a holiday memory has been depicted mainly in cushion and Norwich stitches.*

LONG-LEGGED CROSS STITCH

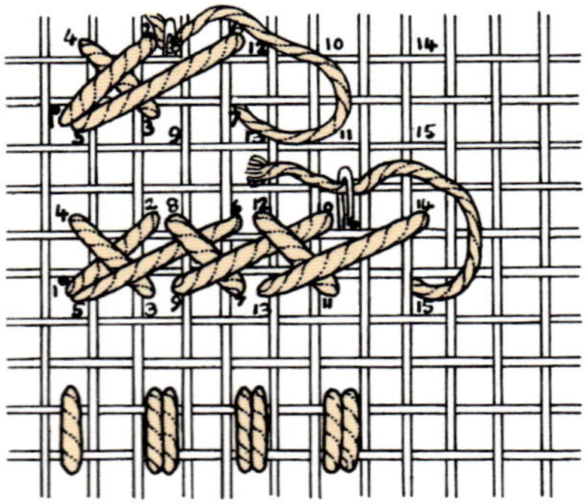

Also known as long-armed cross stitch or plaited Slav stitch, this builds up into a row of lop-sided cross stitches with a plaited effect. Long-legged cross stitch is useful for joining seams, where it gives a braided appearance to the edge, but it requires practice. Start with a small cross stitch over two intersections. This makes a neat beginning, but is not part of the stitch pattern, which moves forward four threads on the first diagonal, and goes back two with the next stitch.

PARISIAN STITCH

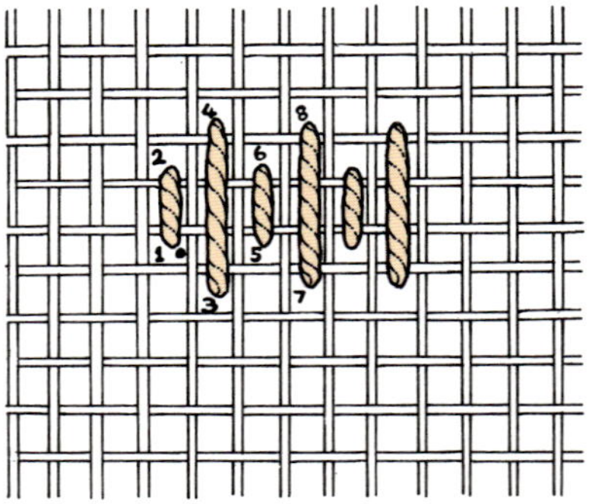

This is a useful filling stitch, or grounding, made up of alternate short and long vertical stitches, over two and four threads, worked horizontally.

HUNGARIAN STITCH

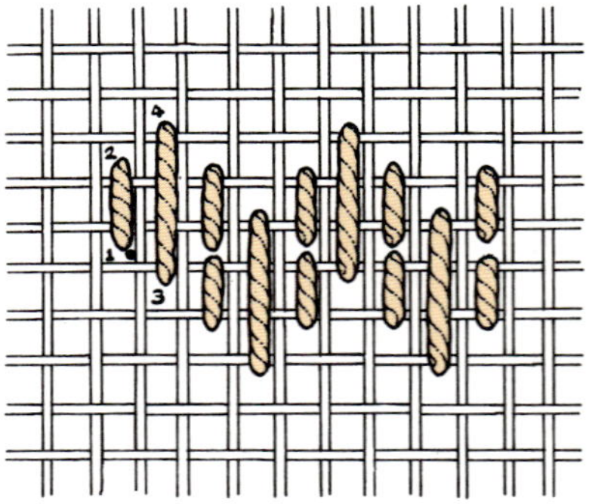

This is worked in a similar way to Parisian stitch, but the stitches are grouped in threes, with a space between each group.

In this first canvas worksheet, Ellen Crawford has experimented with stitches on both a large and a small scale, working on a coloured background with space-dyed threads and fabric strips, as well as with more ordinary materials.

BARGELLO

Also known as Florentine stitch, flame stitch, or point d'Hongrie, Bargello work is the name given to a range of zigzag patterns formed by repeated upright stitches. The stitches are usually worked over four horizontal threads and are stepped, rising and falling by two threads above or below the last. If single stitches are stepped, a pattern of steep peaks is formed: blocks of two or three stitches give gentler curves. You may plan patterns on graph paper or stitch experiments directly on canvas. When creating a pattern, begin in the centre of the first row and work to the end; then return to the centre and make a mirror image, so that you have a matching pattern of repeats. Subsequent rows are stitched from left to right in the usual way.

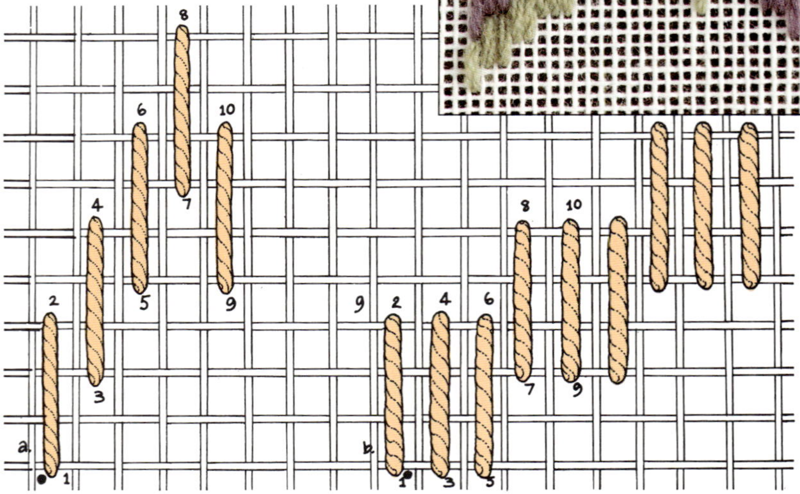

Sweet Peas, by Cecile Forgan, displays a complete mastery of rococo stitch, which is embroidered in three scales. The applied shapes are stitched on nylon gauze.

ROCOCO STITCH

This is a challenging stitch made up of four vertical stitches, over four horizontal threads, into the same holes at the top and bottom, and pulled into a diamond shape by small horizontal stitches. Rococo stitch may be worked on single or double canvas, but on double canvas a regular pattern of holes appears. The thread count is the same in either case.

Rococo stitch is most effective when worked in diagonal rows. The diagram shows the position of the second rococo stitch, two threads down and two to the left of the starting point of the first stitch. The first tying stitch will be worked into the same hole as the base of the first rococo stitch. For clarity the sample has been worked on a large double canvas, counted in the same way.

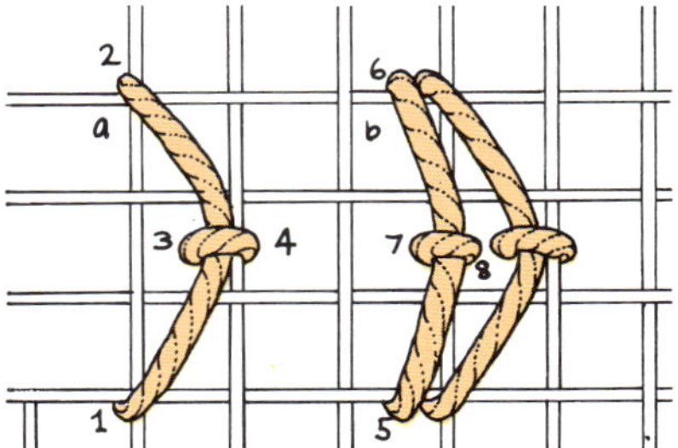

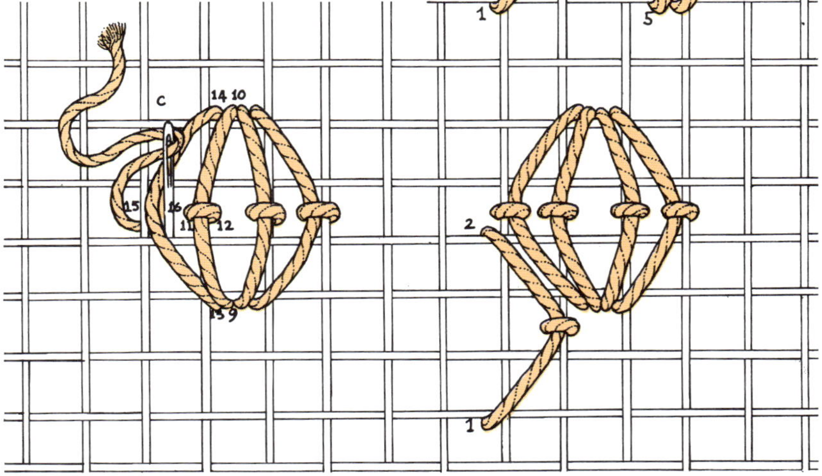

Surface stitches on canvas

Most embroidery stitches may be worked on canvas, especially when it is not necessary to cover the surface completely. They may also be worked on top of a plain area of stitching to give surface interest. Those shown here are only a selection that may inspire further ideas and experiments.

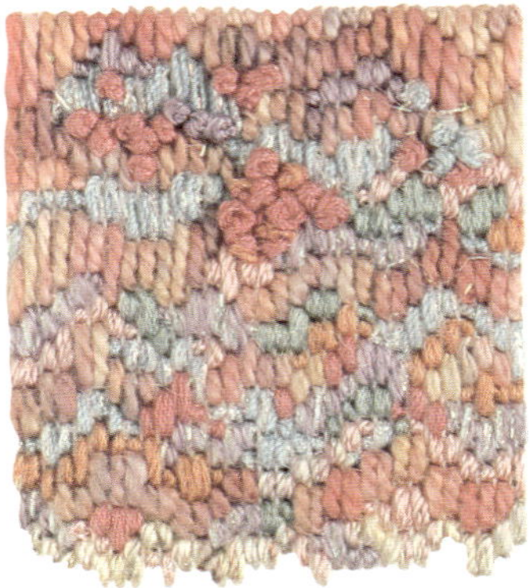

FRENCH KNOTS

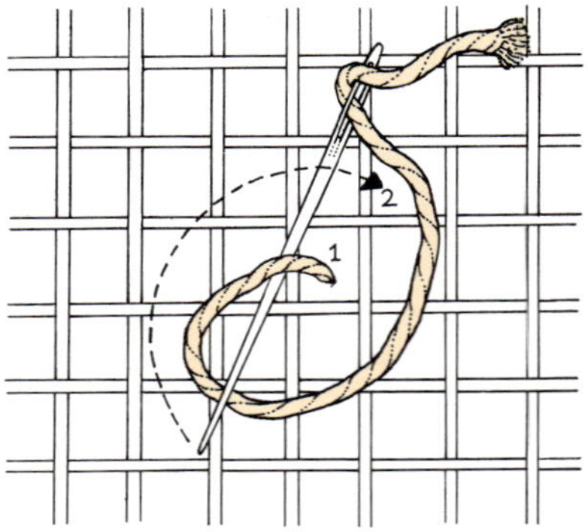

Bring the needle up through the canvas where the knot is needed. Hold the thread between the thumb and forefinger of your left hand, and twist the needle under and then over the thread. Slide this twist up to the canvas intersection; tighten it, and put the needle through on the other side of the intersection.

Simple Florentine stitch experiments by Veronica Long have been embellished with French knots.

BACK STITCH WHEELS

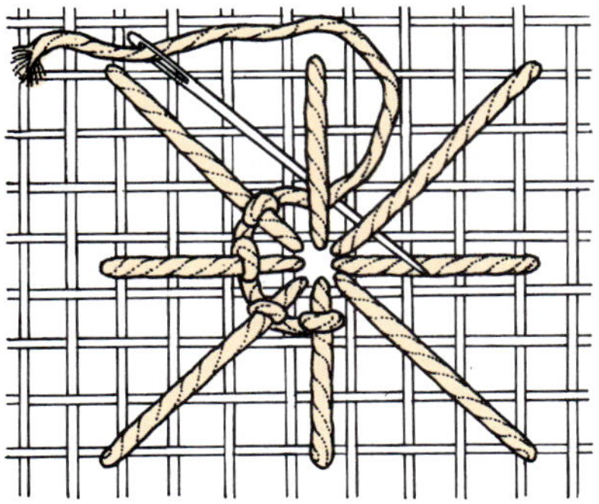

Work a star stitch over a square of an even number of threads. Bring the needle up through the canvas to the left of the vertical stitch at 1, close to the centre of the star. Work a back stitch over that 'arm', passing the needle under it and the next arm; back stitch over that arm, and so on. The needle weaves back over one and forward under two of the surface threads, without going through the canvas. Work rounds until as much of the star as you wish is covered.

CRETAN STITCH

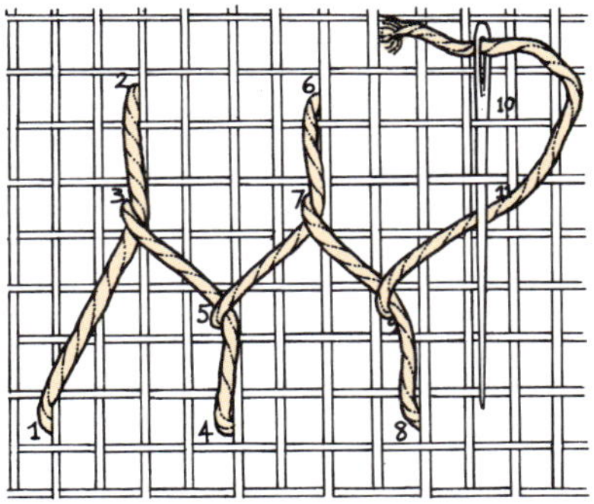

This linear stitch is useful for fillings or for broad lines of varying widths. Always keep the thread to the right of the needle as it enters the fabric to make the short vertical stitches, first at the top (2–3) then at the bottom (4–5) of the line. This very versatile stitch can be worked regularly and closely or freely, both in the spacing and the height of the stitches.

HERRINGBONE STITCH

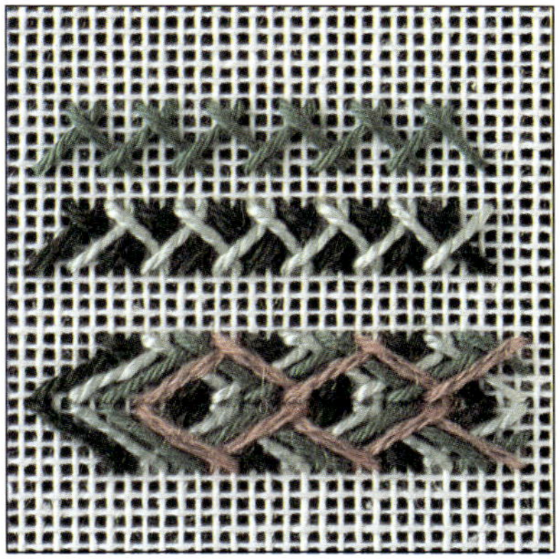

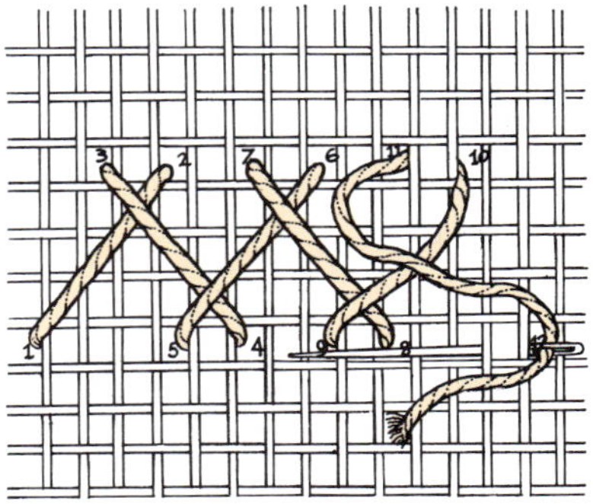

This looks like a row of interlaced cross stitches. The stitches may be of any height or width, and may be worked as regularly or as freely as you wish.

CHAPTER 3

DESIGN METHODS

Simple designs

Design is a word that intimidates some embroiderers, but there are many ways to create your own designs, and several of them are very simple.

Canvas stitches tend to create their own patterns, and you can produce an interesting design simply by changing the size and colour of a stitch, and placing it on the canvas in a variety of shapes. If you encounter problems when trying to stitch curves, change to canvas of a finer mesh. Similarly, tent stitch triangles will have two smooth sides and one ragged side, and again this effect can be diminished by

Shell Purse, *by June Linsley, is embroidered in a free Bargello pattern, using silk, rayon and metallic threads on a coloured nylon mesh, laid on a silver lurex fabric. The design was based on a marbled paper, using the technique shown on page 57. The colours are reminiscent of an abalone shell, which inspired the curved shape of the purse.*

stitching your design on a finer canvas.

Other simple experiments with stitches might entail working some stitches on top of others, an approach which is to be found in other types of modern embroidery. Some needlepoint artists use the simplest stitches to create designs, placing them according to a pattern worked out mathematically.

Simple printing, sponge painting, rubbing, and marbling techniques are other design methods that are worth trying. Continuous practice in drawing eventually pays dividends; at first it may seem difficult and tight and full of mistakes, rather like a child's first attempts at joined-up writing, but drawing will become much easier with practice, until eventually you have developed a style that is fluent and unique.

All these methods have a common need: to exercise and refine the selection process. Design entails making choices about colour, tone, shape, line, texture and composition, and practice makes perfect.

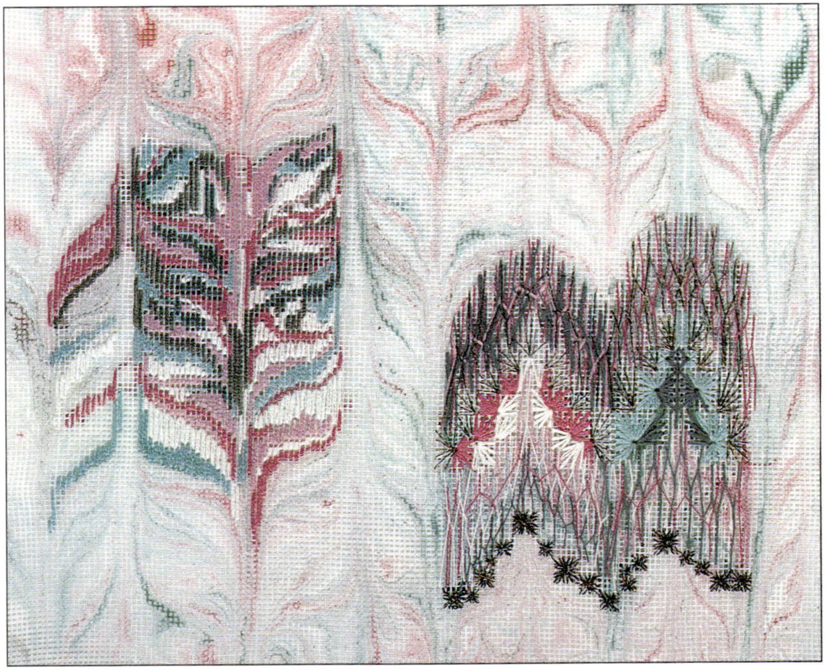

The two Bargello-type patterns shown here have both been taken from the same green and pink design. One pattern has been worked in a traditional manner; the other is more experimental, combining varying weights of thread, and with some stitches laid on top of others.

Using colour

Colour immediately attracts our notice, and plays a strong part in determining whether we like or dislike a design. As embroiderers, we cannot mix colours as if they were paints; we must rely on threads dyed by ourselves or others. Nevertheless, it is necessary to understand how colours work upon each other if we are to produce satisfying results. The canvas grid structure makes it possible to show a very clear line between colours. Alternatively, by using two colours of thread in one needle, a technique that is often impossible on a fine fabric, areas of colour can be merged together.

It is important to use each colour throughout a design, preferably

1 The colour wheel shows the primary colours – red, yellow and blue – and the secondary colours that are made by mixing two primaries. Opposite colours on the wheel are complementary and enhance each other's brilliance, providing they are equal in tone. This contrast may prove useful at the focal point of a design. Neighbouring colours are usually harmonious, since they each contain a proportion of the same colour.

2 Backgrounds can appear to change colours. Try placing the same colour first on a warm background (usually the red/orange/brown range), then on a cool background (blue/green/grey), to see what happens: cool colours will normally recede and warm ones advance.

3 A good range of tone is important in a design, providing areas of contrast. Choose two complementary colours. Mix them together in varied proportions – for example, three blue to one orange, three orange to one blue, and two parts each. Mix white with the complementaries in varying proportions, so that you have two tints of each colour, and three mixtures. These should preferably not be used in the same proportions.

not in areas of equal size. Use one area of the colour to lead the viewer's eye to the next area: this helps to show movement through the design and avoids a spotty, disjointed effect.

By finding colours in the environment and experimenting with them in ways suggested here, you could develop a variety of colour schemes for any purpose. Look not only at natural phenomena, such as skies, plants and animals, but at buildings, hoardings, transport and packaging. Colours are affected by light, so try to select your threads according to the light in which the finished embroidery will be seen. Reflections from shiny threads may be utilized by placing the stitches in different directions.

4 The colours found in a white crocus are shown, first in their correct proportions, then in reverse proportions. Next, these colours are mingled with warm colours, then with cool colours.

5 The colours of a butterfly's wing are arranged according to tone, with the lightest on the left. The same colours are then rearranged as they might be used in a landscape, with the cool colours receding and the warm colours in the foreground appearing to advance.

6 The colours found on an apple are shown first in their correct proportions, then in reverse proportions. Small spots of red and yellow appear to mix, while an intense yellow seems to float on a weaker red and green background.

Repeating patterns (1)

Colour and pattern have been used throughout history to create repeating canvas designs in wool, but many now use pattern in a more abstract way. The pattern in large-scale embroideries today is often created by the use of fabric strips and rug canvas. Others feature canvas grids wrapped with the new metallic threads and combined with areas of bonded lace and fabrics coloured with fabric paints – a far cry from tapestry wool.

Repeated patterns need not fill the whole area of work: they may gradually merge with other less structured areas, or they may change scale. There may be variations within a patterned framework: for example, you might show the different reflections within the more rigid framework of skyscraper windows.

No matter how elaborate or random a pattern may seem, if carefully looked at, it will be found to conform to a pre-planned grid. Only by using a grid can the size and spacing of each part of a pattern be worked out. Since canvas lends itself to a basic rectangular grid, this is the only grid explored here, but there are many more possibilities to be discovered, for example, by referring to the works of Lewis F. Day and William Morris.

Repeating a motif (2, 3, 4)

If you wish to use a motif rather than a geometric shape, the same rules apply. The motif should be placed along the lines of a grid which is equally spaced. The tulip design suggests different ways of repeating a motif. Other variations may be made by contrasting size, colour, and tone, by mixing mat and shiny threads and by mixing outline shapes with silhouettes.

For those who prefer a ready-made pattern, patchwork blocks may be the answer. Complicated patterns can be made from squares, rectangles and triangles, the shapes most easily adapted to canvas-work. Different effects may be obtained with the same shapes, simply by varying the tone. The shapes may be cut out in different coloured papers and moved around until a satisfactory design emerges.

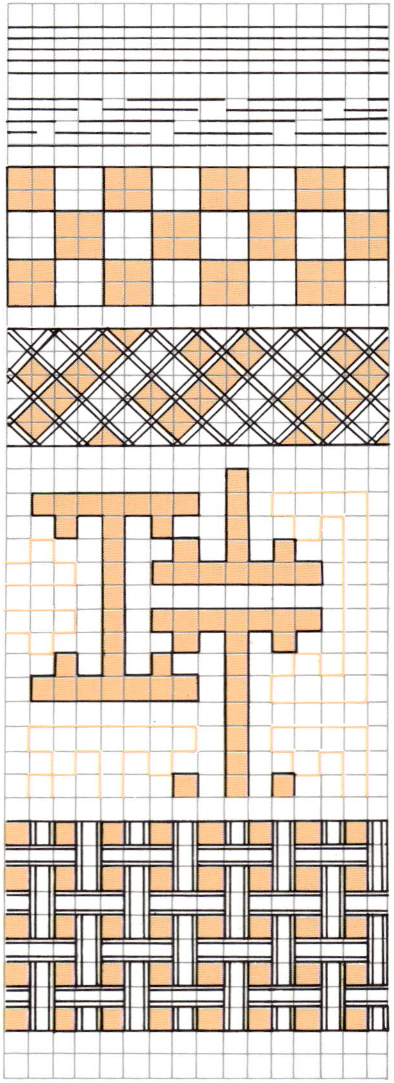

1 Patterns created on a square grid: stripes, broken stripes, a chequer board, a similar chequer pattern turned through 45 degrees, a complex key pattern, and an interlacing pattern.

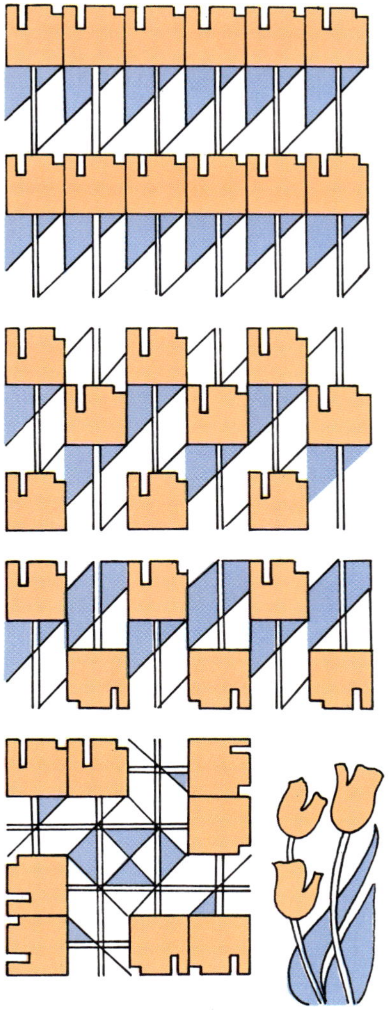

2 A very simple tulip pattern may be interpreted in several ways – with the flowers upright and evenly spaced, at half drop, with alternate rows upside down, or arranged in a square.

3 New patterns emerge when the tones of a patchwork block are changed: top, the construction of the block; below that, a deep tone emphasizes the star, and below that the tones create a column pattern.

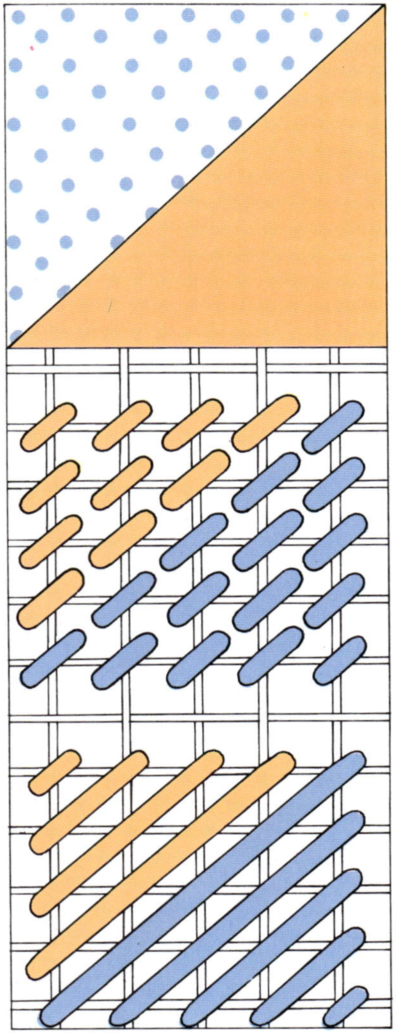

4 It is important to remember that when fabric squares are joined, the pairs of triangles are equal in size, but this is not possible in needlepoint.

Pattern around us

You may not always wish to use patterns which repeat, but set stitches, by their very nature, have a rhythm of their own. Look around and you will find pattern in almost everything: man-made pattern in buildings, for example, or in maps, basket work, or printed and woven fabrics; natural pattern in plants, insects, shells, fish, birds, and minute animal cells. Imagine the various patterns formed by the irregular shape of the Manhattan skyline, fencing and garden gates, formal flower beds, or the climbing plant on a trellis frame. The combination of such patterns and set stitches can often prove

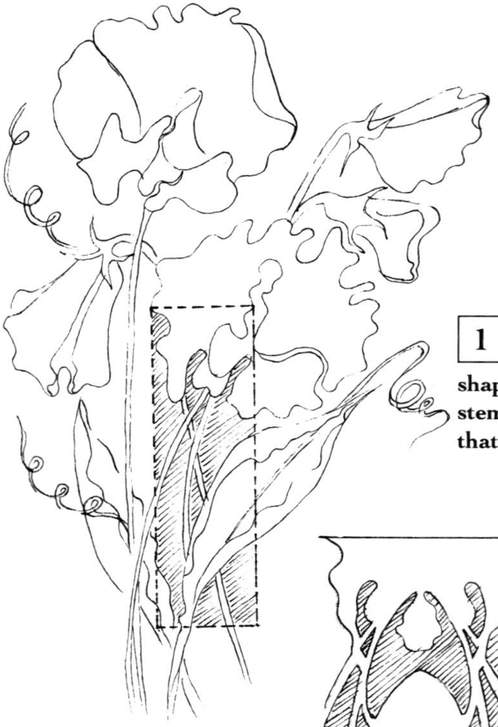

1 **Here, a small area of a drawing is isolated and the shapes between the leaves and the stems are filled in, creating a pattern that could be repeated.**

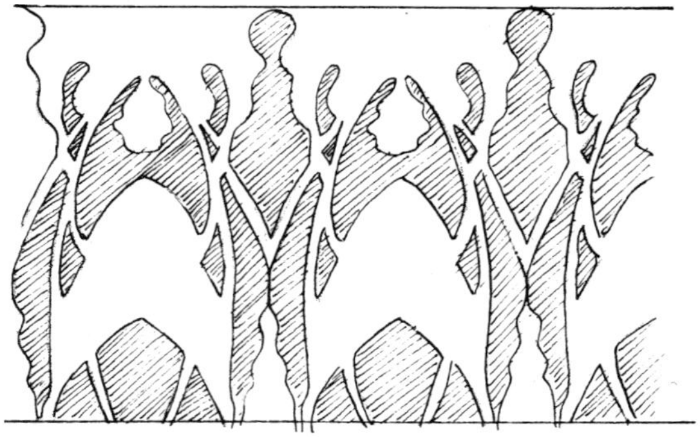

2 **Fields and hedgerows can make an interesting pattern.**

especially successful in canvaswork embroideries.

Look at a subject closely. Find all the basic shapes. Is there a rhythm in the way they are repeated, even if they are not the same size? What are the characteristics of the subject? Can these be emphasized? When you look at the spaces between objects, do they make a pattern you could use?

Try not to let your chosen pattern appear too regular. Make the eye of the onlooker work by putting something where it is least expected. Fill in some shapes and leave others empty, or leave out just enough to stimulate the eye to supply the remainder from imagination.

Here, the repeating tulips design shown on page 47 is used, with changes of scale, and merged with less structured areas.

A canvas embroidery in tent stitch has been created from the patchwork block known as Sherman's March.

Pattern from earlier textiles

Ancient and earlier textiles are a rich source of pattern. It can be very rewarding to spend some time in museums or art galleries where there are many examples of rugs, hangings or clothing, or portraits of people dressed in the clothes and fabrics of past centuries, or where there are collections of folk costumes, particularly those of Asian and Central European peoples.

You may wish to copy a pattern exactly, adapting it to canvas, or it may merely be a starting point for your own ideas. Think also in terms of changing the scale or the colours, or working the pattern in a different texture.

Part of an old Indian textile was used in these embroideries by Jenny Smith. The scale was changed to add interest in one example, while another explores the possibility of creating an ancient, worn look. Neither is a direct copy.

Abstract patterns

Canvas is an excellent medium for abstract patterns, as modern textile artists are beginning to discover. Kate Nicholson, textile designer, has recently been working her designs on canvas. She has this to say about her embroidery:

> 'I trained in textiles at the Royal College of Art. This involved creating both woven and printed textiles. I have always been fascinated by the beauty and rhythms of repeating patterns, and the study of weaving added an interest in the actual mathematical structure of pattern and the effects of light, colour, and tactile quality when using a variety of yarns.
>
> Recent work has been very experimental in all these areas. I like to start with a grid, often very complex and strict – rather like a "ground base" in music – and make my development above this, using ingenuity, wit and a personal way of seeing, which has been termed lyrical.'

White Flower, *by Kate Nicholson, is an abstract plant design in beige and white, made with tent stitch.*

Coloured Fragments, *again by Kate Nicholson, is also in tent stitch. Here, the pattern grid on the left gradually changes structure and colour, reversing itself completely by the time the right-hand side is reached. Patterns such as this require to be very carefully worked out, in colour, on graph paper.*

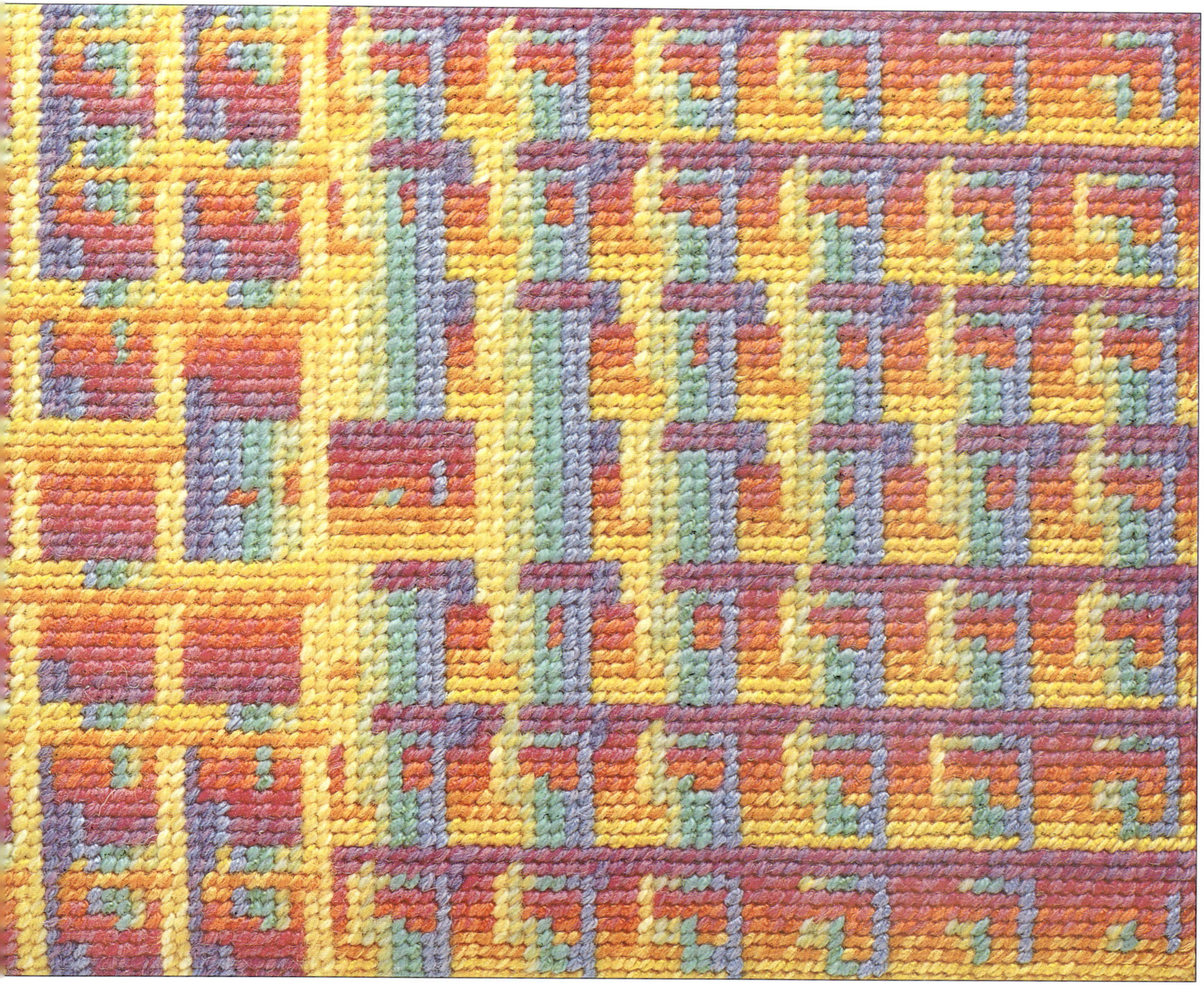

A tissue paper collage

If you do not enjoy drawing you may prefer this way of designing, which interprets a subject in blocks of colour rather than graphically. The semi-transparent nature of tissue paper makes it possible to build up mixtures of colour where papers overlap, even though the picture only uses three or four different colours of paper.

Begin by studying your chosen subject. Carefully observe the colours, and the graduations of shades and tones of colour. Choose tissue papers in these colours and tear them up into small irregular pieces about 2.5cm (1in.) square, arranging them into separate piles. All you need apart from this is a sheet of background paper, cold-water paste and brush, and two L-shaped pieces of card, as shown.

1 Cover the area of background paper to be used with cold-water paste. Working quickly and spontaneously, select pieces of tissue in the desired colour and place them on the background, as if you were painting the subject. Repaste the background paper if it dries. Keep the tissue flat, do not screw it up.

2 Overlap the pieces as you work, trying to achieve variations in tone and mixtures of colour where one colour overlaps another. Do not work minutely in one small area at a time but work over the whole piece simultaneously. This will give more movement to the finished design.

3 Consider the finished work, looking for balance of shape, line, colour, tone and movement. You can adjust pieces at this stage. Using windows made from two L-shaped pieces of card, place them over different parts of the collage and select an area to embroider. If you are stitching the whole collage, lay the framing pieces on the outer boundaries of the collage to check that it sits well in the frame.

card frame has been used to solate and identify areas of a issue paper collage of delphiniums nd pink daisies.

llen Crawford has translated nother area more simply, using arisian stitch.

A finely embroidered piece in tent stitch, by Pen Smith, echoes the merging of colours where papers on the collage are overlapped.

A third area is worked in irregular Gobelin stitches. The isolated triangular shape may be rotated through 360 degrees to create a circular design.

Marbling for Bargello

Beautiful marbled papers, originally used for endpapers and book binding, are available commercially. They provide lovely ideas for Bargello embroidery, but they are very expensive. It is much cheaper to make your own marbled papers, as described here. You might find inspiration for colour schemes in various rock crystals: the layers of colour would correspond well to Bargello patterns.

It is advisable to have plenty of paper, such as bond or typing paper, and ample space in which to lay the patterns out to dry. In addition, you will need a shallow tray filled with cold wallpaper paste; either oil paints and white spirit and containers in which to mix them, or ready mixed commercial marbling ink; artists' paint brushes for each colour, and a spare brush or orange sticks with which to stroke the pattern. Remember that the paints will mix in use, producing other colours; for example, yellow and blue will mix to produce green.

These patterns were made by the marbling method. Some are on paper, while others have been made directly on canvas, which is then ready to stitch.

1 Fill a tray with wallpaper paste, made up to a thick pouring consistency. Mix marbling ink or oil paint to a milky consistency with white spirit. Load your brush with colour and dot the ink either at random or with regular spacing, just on the surface of the paste. The dots should be no larger than the size of a small coin.

2 Stroke a clean brush through the surface of the paste, first one way and then the other. A pattern will appear on the paste; do not continue to comb for too long or the colours may turn muddy.

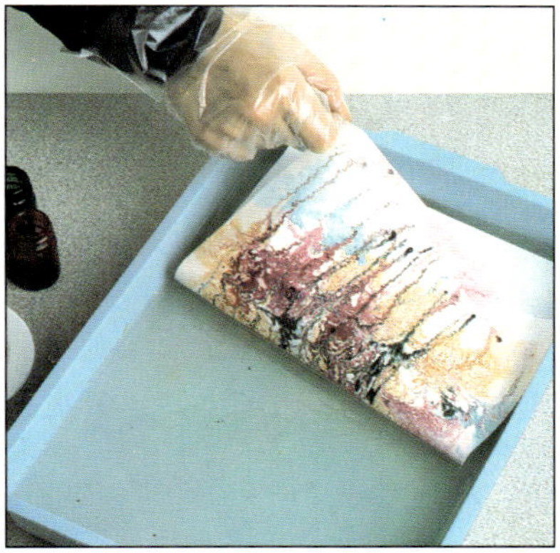

3 Lower a piece of paper on the surface of the paste, taking care not to trap any air bubbles. The paper will pick up the pattern and the surplus paste should then be gently rinsed off under cold running water.

Because the colours are oil-based, the pattern will stay on the paper, which must be laid out flat to dry. If you try the method directly on canvas, allow more time for the canvas to pick up the pattern, as the sizing in the canvas will resist the ink a little. The paste should be gently rinsed off before drying. It is essential to lay the canvas flat to dry or to pin it out on a board so that it does not dry with a distorted weave.

It is possible to marble canvas directly, but care must be taken, first that you do not let the canvas sink under the paste, and secondly that you give the canvas more time to pick up the pattern before very carefully washing off the paste (it is easy to wash the pattern off with the paste).

Simple methods for abstract design

Paper strip weaving (1, 2)

The idea behind this method is to produce interesting blocks of colour in an abstract design. The blocks of colour will have variations in tone and pattern, yet still fall within the grid framework which is most useful for canvas embroidery.

Choose coloured pictures from magazines, selecting those that look as if they might combine to offer an interesting range of colour and tone. Try to include some plain papers and, at first, avoid pictures that have a great deal of small detail. These may look well when woven into a design but will be very difficult to translate into embroidery.

1 **Cut plain and patterned colour pages into strips of varied width, ranging from 1cm (3/8in.). Select some strips that look attractive together. Start with a central area or motif, and place strips all around, randomly mixing patterns with plains. Manoeuvre the strips around until you are happy with the design.**

2 **Place the strips on a clean background paper and weave them or just lay them around the central strip in your chosen design, holding them in place with masking tape. Select an interesting area to reproduce on canvas.**

Potato block printing (3, 4)

With potato block printing, you will find yourself making decisions: where to place a colour or shape; how large a block to use; whether to overlap one colour on top of another; whether to press the blocks lightly so that there are some patches that are barely covered, or whether to flood the block with colour so that the paint oozes out and makes patterns on its own. Ideas for colours could be taken from flowers or a weathered brick wall. The first would probably lead to a clear, bright colour scheme, while the other would produce a more subtle and subdued blend of colours.

The patterns that you create may be transferred to canvas simply as blocks of colour, formed by two or three stitches, or you may see a resemblance to man-made or natural forms, or even to people!

Using the oval-rectangle-verticals recipe, given overleaf, for human figures, you can create distinct characters, like this old woman, who was printed with pieces of potato and thick poster paints.

3 **Choose your colours: poster paint mixed with dilute water-based glue works well. Cut a potato into simple rectangles, squares or strips. Try to keep an even surface on the potato. Either paint the colour onto the surface of the block or dip the block into paint which has been poured onto a pad and print it on your background paper.**

4 **Try to maintain a good balance in tone and shape, and avoid making the design too bitty. Sometimes allow one colour to dry before printing the next one; at other times, print a second colour while the first is still wet, so that the two merge at the edges. You can print colours on top of one another, so that the underlying colour shows through.**

Figures

If you do not draw very well you will probably be dismayed at the idea of embroidering figures. Detailed portraits and photographs with three-dimensional effects will come into your mind, but such exact reproductions are not the province of embroidery. Think, instead, of the stylized matchstick men of L. S. Lowry or of other naive artists, and consider the economy with which cartoonists convey the idea of the human form.

It is a liberating notion to realize that a combination of an oval, a long rectangle, two verticals for legs, and possibly two horizontals, will read as a person. Untrained artists in sophisticated and in primitive societies use this recipe, as do children, and you can also have fun experimenting with it. The shapes may be doodled or scribbled freehand – perhaps when you are sitting in a car watching people in a queue – or you might use potato block printing. Alternatively, you might find it easier to trace an outline from a photograph or magazine, or even simply cut shapes out and use them as templates.

When you have satisfactory shapes, enlarge them, if necessary. You may choose either to transfer them directly to canvas, or to plan a chart on graph paper, before you begin stitching. The obvious choices for figures – tent stitch or satin stitch – will give different effects. The finished effect does not have to be naturalistic, so enjoy experimenting with both form and colour.

Simplified shapes, doodled from a photograph of children, were transferred to graph paper and worked in satin stitch.

A photograph of running figures was traced from a newspaper photograph and successive outlines were overlapped. They were then crayonned in short diagonal strokes, with alternating thick and thin layers to help to suggest movement.

This is part of a small panel by Stella Chandler, who began the work when a complete beginner. It is a personal record of a new hobby, and details of dress, stance and equipment are correct. Using the figure recipe, Ambitious Bowlers *was first charted on graph paper and then stitched.*

Design from observation

One of the reasons for the emphasis on drawing in design is that drawing sharpens the powers of observation. The finished drawing may be mediocre, or even bad, but while you have been using pencil or crayons, you have been concentrating on the subject much more intensely than you might otherwise have been. You have recorded small details that might have escaped notice – tiny shapes, variations of texture and unusual combinations of colour.

The work that follows comes from a class drawing session based on fish. Detailed still-life drawings were not the object of the exercise, but students were asked to concentrate on the patterns of the scales and details of eyes, fins and tails. As a result of the concentration required by drawing fish patterns, a great deal of information had been gathered, and the students then worked directly on the canvas, using a variety of threads.

For the fin, Sheila Shaw used random straight stitches and sequins on a lightly coloured canvas. A heavily stitched background area in white straight stitches gives, by contrast, a lightness to the fin area.

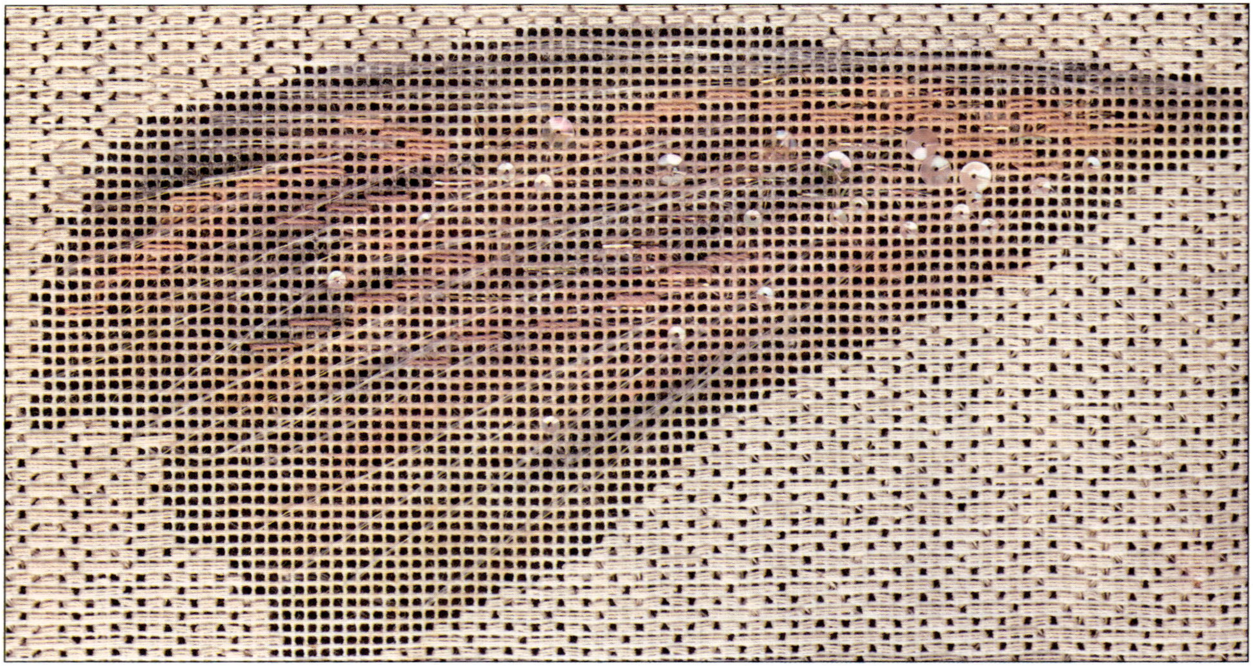

The eye of the fish has been worked by Janet Edmonds in velvet stitch, using wool and fabric strips.

To create the tail, Janet Edmonds grafted a fine tent-stitched section onto coarser canvas, which was embroidered with straight stitches and lengths of fine thread trimmed with beads.

The scales may be depicted in a variety of ways: here, straight stitches have been worked on black and silver square mesh mounted on canvas (Sheila Shaw).

An evening bag by Sheila Shaw uses colours and shapes derived from the study of fish scales. It is worked on 22-mesh canvas in tent stitch, using fine silk threads and an iridescent thread.

Breaking up a landscape

There are so many confusing images in a landscape that it is advisable to use a window made by cutting a rectangular hole in a postcard. This will enable you to mask excess detail.

Having selected your view it is helpful to make a few quick sketches to find the best composition and ask yourself a few questions. Is it a busy scene full of small fields, buildings or hedgerows? If so, you may wish to have a low horizon so that a large, relatively empty sky provides a feeling of space. Are there charming pockets of detail on which you would like to concentrate, forsaking the horizon altogether? Is there a feature, such as a fence, a lane or the furrows of a ploughed field, that would lead the eye into the scene? If so, how could you make the most of it?

Is there a good range of tone, or lightness or darkness which you could utilize to give interest and contrast at a vital spot? Is there pattern? For instance, hillsides covered in evergreens are a rich source of pattern, as we see the tops dance up and down and around the contours of the hills. Are similar shapes – sometimes large, sometimes small – repeated throughout the scene? Is there interest in the foreground, where you would be able to develop textural detail?

Most important of all, why choose this particular scene? What are the features that attract you and which do you wish to emphasize?

Your quick sketches could show the horizon at different levels, or features in different places, or show where 'mass' such as clumps of trees, or buildings, or mountains, would be in relation to the 'space' of sky or plain. Avoid placing a feature in the exact centre of a scene, as this has the effect of chopping it in half. Avoid, too, having an even ratio of mass to space or busy areas to empty areas. Practise discrimination at all times, in order to gain a satisfying balance.

Reduce buildings to basic blocks and triangles. Find symbols to suggest trees – children do this automatically, making lollipop trees, or trees with branches sticking out straight at each side of an upright trunk in a very decorative way. Many abstract artists work in this way. You are not aiming to copy painting but to exploit the special qualities of canvas structure and interesting threads.

A series of quick sketches of a scene shows a slightly different viewpoint, focal point or horizon line and varying amounts of filled and open space.

A more detailed sketch of the chosen scene shows pattern and rhythm of line, with areas of contrasting tone, and suggests foreground detail and texture.

The design uses set canvas stitches for the most part, applying them in a rhythmic way. Some threads have been withdrawn from a separate piece of canvas, wrapped on the machine, and then applied to the embroidery. Free straight stitches have been used in places.

Presentation

Embroiderers of earlier times usually close-framed their finished needlepoint, the stitching meeting the edges of the frame. This is still often done, especially when a small first piece has been finished – once the initial excitement is over, it is natural to want to see your work framed and displayed. On the other hand, when you consider how much time has been devoted to the stitching of even a small piece, it is worth giving some thought to alternative methods of presentation. You might, for example, enhance the piece by allowing space around the embroidery, rather than cramming it in a frame. With experience, you will give thought to this at the design stage or at least during the working of your project.

Professional framers will give advice on the choice of moulding for the frame and the colour of any inner card mount, but they may not be aware of other options available. If you have a commercially cut mount, ensure that the lower margin is slightly deeper than those at the top and the sides, otherwise the embroidery may appear to fall out of the bottom of the frame.

If you have left the background canvas partly unworked, there are a number of alternatives. You need to decide, then, on the area of canvas to be framed; whether to use a card or fabric-covered window mount; whether to allow an area of slightly stitched canvas to be seen; whether embroidered borders should be added, or whether a padded frame should be made. And, of course, the choice of colour for any surround is of paramount importance, both with regard to the embroidery itself and to the room in which it will be hung.

Before you remove the embroidery from the working frame, decide on its most effective size. This can best be done with two L-shaped pieces of card, laid on the canvas to form a square or rectangle. At this point, try to get some preliminary ideas about the colour of mount by laying different coloured papers or fabric pieces around the embroidery. Be adventurous in this: do not rely on preconceived ideas.

Do not remove the embroidery from the working frame until you are ready to stretch it, if this is necessary, and you have chosen the final method of framing.

1 The sprayed background canvas has been broken by lines of machine satin stitch, but lines of darning would work equally well. A close frame – a narrow dull gold moulding, which matches the flower centres – is considered first.

2 To give the embroidery space, a larger frame with a card mount may be used. Here, a silver frame, matching the machined lines, is tried with a dark grey mount. A green mount would seem the obvious choice, but it would be difficult to match the green canvas, and might give too green an effect.

3 Canvas darned with fabric strips is considered as an alternative. To mask the join, an inner frame worked on plastic canvas is used.

4 Sometimes the most unexpected choices work. The dark red card mount enhances both the purple and the green, and the square striped frame works well with it.

CHAPTER 4

SPECIAL EFFECTS

Of the enormous range of new fabrics and threads being developed today, there are few that are specifically designed for canvaswork: plastic canvas and the washable plasticized rug canvases appear to be the only exceptions. But there are many ways of giving a new look to traditional canvases: you might, for example, widen the spectrum of threads you choose, or combine canvas with other kinds of embroidery.

You may choose to leave part of your canvas unworked or to colour it in some way, so that it plays a positive part in the design. Canvas may be distorted or moulded from its flat state, or have parts cut away to reveal worked areas at different levels and with different scales of stitching. The cut-away pieces may be coloured or stitched, and re-applied on top, giving a multi-layered effect. You might decide to substitute an entirely different background, such as fine square-meshed nylon net or gauze, or the kind of coarse metal mesh intended for gardening or constructional use.

In addition to selecting from the wide and varied range of metallic threads and the exciting new knitting yarns (which may be coaxed through the canvas), you might dye threads yourself for a special project. These give a subtlety of colour which is difficult to achieve otherwise. You might make new threads by combining existing ones into fine cords by hand or machine. These may either be used for stitching (or coarser canvas) or be couched down on top of finer canvases.

Georgina Rees began Turkish Carpets *by arranging squares and triangles of embroidered plastic canvas on a coloured canvas. She then added squares of machine embroidery and linked these areas with lines of darning and formal stitchery. Much of the canvas is left unstitched, its grid being emphasized by the green lurex fabric on which it is mounted.*

Plastic canvas

Plastic canvas with its fairly coarse grid of 10, 7 or 5 points, meshes or threads to the inch is one of the few new materials for canvaswork. It is widely obtainable in pre-formed sheets and a limited number of shapes – circles, squares and diamonds – intended for use in box-making. As it has been available for only a few years, we do not know how it will age, but nevertheless it is interesting to experiment with this new material.

Many serious embroiderers are deterred by its coarse mesh, which makes most conventional needlepoint stitches look clumsy, and by its plastic feel. On the positive side, it is useful for children who are learning to embroider, for those who find finer canvas tiring to the eyes, and for teachers making class samples that will be handled a great deal. And it has many other advantages: the mesh does not distort, so you will not need to use a frame and your work will be easy to transport; the plastic is semi-rigid and can easily be cut into shapes that will not fray, so it is useful for constructed pieces and free-

To make Squares, *Rosemary Jacquin took squares of plastic canvas and darned and wrapped them with fine ribbons, fabric strips and perlé threads. They were then assembled on rug canvas in an abstract pattern. The colour scheme is based on poppies.*

1 **To begin, double the thread, putting both ends through the needle. Pass the needle through the mesh, back over the edge and through the loop. Work the next stitch into the next mesh. Sew with one or both ends.**

2 **Cover the edges of the mesh, using a thick thread. Work two or three stitches into each mesh. The stitches should fan out to cover the edge completely.**

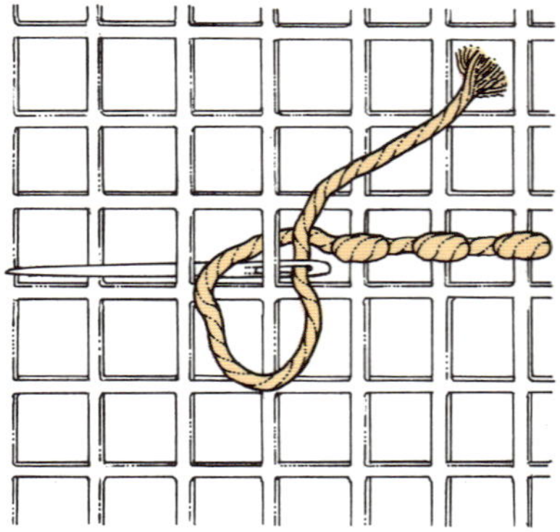

3 **Back stitch may be used to fill in the central area. As the fine thread does not fill the mesh, the back of the stitch can be seen as a shadow.**

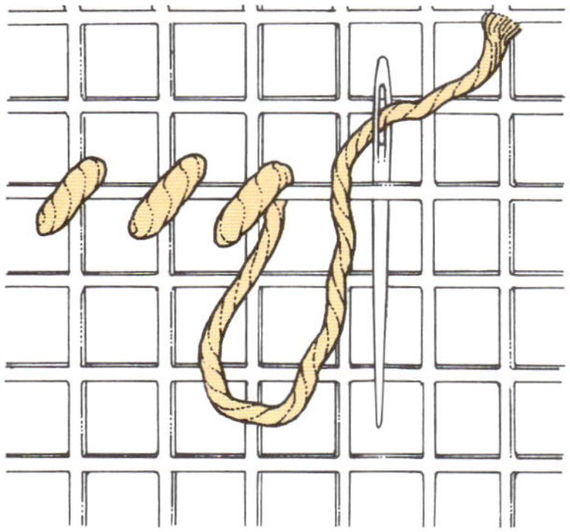

4 **Half cross stitch is an alternative filling. Return 'journeys' may be made with thread of a different colour.**

hanging objects, and it can also be used as an unseen strengthening in constructional techniques for which cardboard would not be suitable.

In addition to these practical advantages, the plastic mesh has a translucent quality that can be enhanced by stitching with very fine threads: machine embroidery thread, for example, can give a very delicate shadow of colour. In general, silky and shiny threads are preferable to wool.

Embroidering a small shape

Small square or oblong shapes are easiest to start with, and you can use these first experiments for earrings, pendants and hair-slides, for Christmas tree decorations, or for parts of a mobile. Several, laid side by side, will give you the idea for a larger embroidery of applied shapes, in this way providing another method of designing.

Select a group of fine threads in a pleasing colour combination: you might take the colours from a shell or a flower, for example, or choose them to match a purse or some other accessory. Stranded

Plastic canvas is easily shaped into earrings, pendants, beads or hair ornaments (all by June Linsley).

cotton is a good thread to use, and may be combined with fine metallic threads.

Cut a shape – perhaps a square of seven or eight threads. Trim the nubbed edges until they are smooth. If you are covering the edges, either overcasting or an even buttonhole stitch, using up to six strands of embroidery cotton will create a neat edge.

Next, fill the main part of the grid with half cross or back stitch, working back and forwards, or circling round into the centre. Finer threads may be used here to create a jewelled quality. Work several layers of stitches in different colours, or use one colour horizontally and one vertically. Eyelets or Norwich stitch may also be used.

Try to keep the back of the piece as neat as possible, especially if you are making jewellery. Finish by running the thread through existing stitches and securing the end with a small dab of glue.

Manipulating canvas

So far we have considered using canvas only in a two-dimensional way, but need it be just a flat surface? Canvas is a fairly rigid fabric, capable of maintaining a three-dimensional shape without any supporting padding, at least over a small area.

Some ways of distorting or manipulating the canvas are explored here: it can be twisted, pushed up over acrylic rods or knitting needles into wave patterns, or pleated in either flat pleats or zig-zags, and it can be moulded over various forms when wet, and left to dry. The moulds may be anything from bowls or saucers to armatures of galvanized chicken wire or papier mâché, or even, for small areas, of moulded tissues. Strips of canvas can also be held down with stitches in some areas and pushed up elsewhere. Canvas can be formed into cone shapes and cylinder shapes. In all cases, you will find that it is easier to work the stitching on the flat canvas before distorting the surface.

Phyllis Gunstone worked straight stitches around cutwork squares, rather in the manner of Hardanger embroidery. Eyelets were stitched at each corner and crosses wrapped over each square. The canvas was then pleated, accordion style, and machine-made braids were looped across the design.

A drawing of a reflection in water was rendered in straight stitches. The embroidery was then pushed up over thin rods, emphasizing the wave-like design.

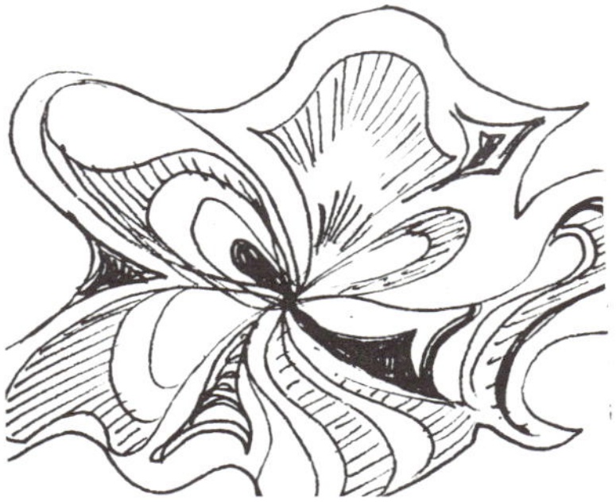

Two canvas manipulation experiments were used by Peggy Field for this box. A reflection in a distorted mirror was used for the lid: smooth tent stitch and Gobelin stitches were worked in sparkly machine threads and stranded embroidery cotton. The stitched canvas was then thoroughly soaked in cold water; moulded into shape over packed tissues, and held down at the edges with thumb tacks into the base board. When it was dry, the bead was attached, and the lid was lined.

The design for the body of the box was also based on a reflection, again with plain and shimmering threads, but this time using machine satin stitch of varying widths to evoke the image of choppy water. The flat strip of stitched canvas was lined; stitched down at irregular intervals to a straight strip of covered canvas, and pushed out between the rows of stitching. A base and lining finished the box.

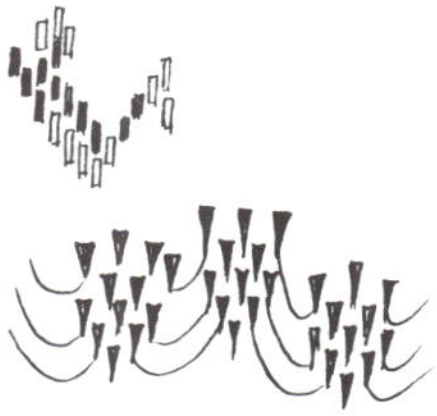

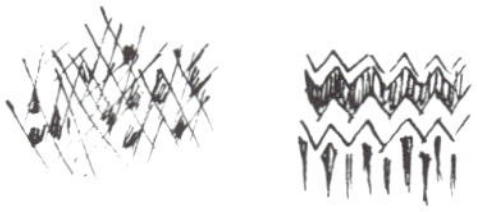

To create the bird, Peggy Field first made a paper pattern, to determine how much canvas would be taken up by the pleating. A flat canvas shape of the bird was cut as a base, and the head was worked on this. A separate body was stitched and mounted on the base in a slightly raised cone shape. The wings were first embroidered, then pleated, before being attached to the base shape. Tassels and cords represent the feet. Gobelin, leaf and fly stitches and diamond eyelets were used.

Painting and spraying the canvas

A plain white canvas can be coloured in some way to match the colour scheme that you intend to use. Any dye or paint that is likely to run if the finished work has to be damp stretched is best avoided: the colour would bleed into the thread. Acrylic paints, however, even when they are diluted with water, are permanent when dry.

There are a number of fabric paints on the market which will colour the canvas well. Most manufacturers recommend washing the fabric before painting and then ironing to make the colour fast, but care needs to be taken with canvas. Do not wash it: pin it carefully over absorbent paper on a board before painting; leave it to dry thoroughly, with pins or thumb tacks still in place, and then, to make the colour permanent, cover the pinned canvas with a cloth and iron it according to the instructions. After ironing, leave the canvas fixed to the board for about 24 hours, to allow the size to reset.

Small cans of aerosol spray paint, designed for retouching cars, may also be used, and there are now spray paints that are environ-

1 Cut a shape from a piece of cardboard, taking care not to damage the outline. If you cut carefully along the outline, this will produce a negative stencil and a positive template.

2 The stencil is sprayed through carefully masking the other areas. When this is dry the stencil is moved to the next position and sprayed through again. Make sure the stencil is dry before using it again.

3 Templates are held to the canvas with double-sided sticky tape. A negative shape is left after the background around them has been sprayed.

A simplified stencil of an onion flower head was sprayed on the canvas and used as a guide for stitching this small panel. Eyelets, Rhodes stitch, darning and tassels have been used. Part of the canvas is left unworked to show the use of the stencil.

mentally safe. Work out of doors to avoid inhaling the spray, and either use stencils or simply colour the background. Instead of applying a single background colour, you might like to merge two or three colours to provide a more interesting area on which to stitch.

Stencils and templates

You may choose to spray the background before using a stencil. Normally the fabric paint is applied through the stencil with either a stencil brush or a sponge, but it is simpler to use an airbrush or car spray. If you move the stencil a little after each spraying, a more complex, oversprayed design may emerge. The stencil may be placed at any angle, and even rotated through a circle. In fact it can become a creative tool. If it is held a little above the surface of the canvas, a softer edge may be produced.

Experiment with ideas, always trying them out on paper to begin with. You might, for example, cut a simple stencil to follow the horizon of a landscape. The sky could be sprayed with the lower half in position, and the earth with the upper half masking the sky.

Space dyeing your threads

This is an inexpensive and easy way to acquire a range of shaded and variegated threads in coordinating colours. Start with the basic method, as outlined here, then experiment with other groups of contrasting colours. If possible, keep an accurate record of the exact kinds and quantities of dyes used, and the types and shades of thread, together with a small length of each yarn, both before and after dyeing. The cold-water dyes used for space dyeing cannot satisfactorily be used with acrylic or polyester fibres, nor with ordinary embroidery wool, but you can achieve excellent results with the following: silk threads – both embroidery and knitting yarns; cotton threads – stranded or perlé embroidery threads or cotton knitting yarn; rayon/viscose fashion yarns; linen – both embroidery and fashion knitting yarns; machine-washable knitting wool, and even ribbons and fabric strips in white or pastel shades (again, these should be woven from natural fibres or viscose, not polyester).

Different fibres will be differently affected by the dye, and the final results will also depend on the initial colour of the thread or yarn, so you will end up with a range of shaded and variegated threads, all of which will coordinate. This can be particularly useful for adding richness and subtlety to an area of stitching. If you wish to convey the range of greens in grass or foliage, for example, you might choose to dye your threads with blues, yellows and a green mixed from the two, which would intermingle and overlay each other.

To gain a comparable effect with commercial yarns, you would need to change the colour of your thread every two or three stitches, and sometimes use two threads in the needle at the same time. So time spent on the dyeing process will be more than saved on the stitching.

Preparation

Use cold-water dyes, sometimes referred to as fibre-reactive or Procion dyes. It is economical to start with the primary colours – red, yellow and blue – since these can be mixed to achieve other colours, and if you consistently use the same red, yellow and blue your threads will always match.

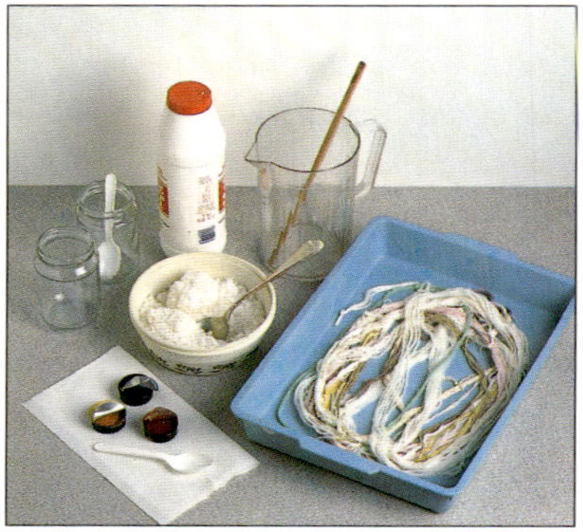

1 **Choose a selection of threads and yarns and, perhaps, ribbons and fabric strips, taking about a seven metre (eight yard) length of each. Wind each length into a long hank, tying it loosely to prevent tangling. Soak the hanks in water for an hour; then squeeze out the excess water, and lay the hanks around the edges of a shallow tray or dish.**

2 Spoon the dyes at intervals over the threads, allowing the colours to overlap and merge. If the dye colours seem too strong for your purpose, they may be diluted, but remember that the colours will appear much paler when dry. Leave the hanks as they are for between five and ten minutes, then check that the dyes have penetrated through to the underlying threads.

3 Dilute the concentrated soda solution by mixing about 40ml (between two and three tablespoons) of soda solution to a litre (1¾pt.) of water, and pour the solution gently over the threads, covering them completely. Do not stir or prod the contents, which will appear a brownish colour. Leave them for at least 30 minutes to fix the dyes.

4 Pour away the liquid and rinse the threads thoroughly. Wash them in detergent and warm water, then leave them to dry. When the threads have dried, wind them on cardboard rolls. Clean all the equipment thoroughly.

You will also require a few shallow containers, such as plastic trays or baking trays; jars to hold dye and other solutions; a measuring jug; measuring spoons, and cooking salt and washing soda.

Prepare a concentrated salt solution: about 50g (2oz.) salt to 300ml (½pt.) of hot water. Also prepare a concentrated solution of about 100g (4oz.) washing soda in 450ml (¾pt.) of hot water. (These amounts are approximate.)

Using a jar as a container, mix a level half teaspoon of dye powder with a tablespoon of salt solution. Add hot water until the jar is half full, stirring until all the dye is dissolved. Repeat the process to make as many dye colours as you want. Once mixed, the dyes have an effective life of up to four hours. Do not try to store dyes; throw away any surplus at the end of the session.

Space-dyed threads are used for the adaptation of cushion stitch chosen for the brickwork, for the velvet-stitched leaves and for the French-knot flowers.

Left *In each of the small panels shown here, two canvases, with different mesh sizes, are used.*

Four space-dyed threads are used together in the needle to darn these bricks. Finer threads are used for the eyelet flowers (top left).

Strips of space-dyed fabric are darned through rug canvas for this brickwork (bottom left).

Space-dyed threads give subtle colour variations for the sky, fields and flowers of Landscape, *by Diana Dawson. One or two commercially dyed wools are used for contrast.*

CHAPTER 5

CANVAS AND OTHER EMBROIDERY TECHNIQUES

If you use canvas for techniques not usually associated with it, you may achieve interesting results. Machining on canvas, for example, will produce quite different effects from machining on more usual fabrics, and this provides a relatively new area for experiments.

It is worth spending time thinking creatively about different ways in which you can use canvas. For example, think of it as just another piece of evenweave fabric, remembering that woven canvas has different possibilities from interlock canvas. The movable threads of woven canvas can be pulled tightly together, re-aligned or withdrawn completely. It may therefore be used for drawn thread, needleweaving and pulled work, amongst other techniques. The open weave also enables laid work and other techniques to be explored more easily. The non-fraying quality of interlock and plastic canvas could add a new dimension to appliqué and cutwork.

Surprisingly, you will find that many apparently new ideas have in fact been tried before, but have then been forgotten or set aside. This is why looking at old embroideries and a little personal research will often give valuable starting points for individual work. For example, the Victorians embroidered a kind of blackwork on canvas, calling it 'canvas lace'. They also produced embroideries on paper and on metal mesh (most of which have now, unfortunately, rusted away), and their canvaswork samplers show charming examples of surface stitches on canvas. Yet, sadly, it is the image of their coarse Berlin wool work that has survived.

Jennie Parry stitched this panel, Impressions from Seurat, *entirely by machine. Using a regular, jerky movement, she made two or three narrow zigzag stitches (stitch width 2–2½) into each pair of holes of the 10-mesh canvas. Most of the stitching was worked horizontally, though the reeds in the centre were worked vertically. The tailor tacking foot was used for the foreground, with two threads in the needle. Multi-coloured rayon threads were used, with the addition of some invisible and metallic threads.*

Machining on canvas

Many people do not realize that it is possible to machine on canvas, both with controls at normal, and with the adaptations necessary for free machine embroidery. A whole panel may be worked by machine on canvas; you can combine areas of machine stitching with hand stitching, or you may cover the canvas with a wash of machine-stitched colour or pattern before adding extra decoration, such as hand embroidery, applied fabrics, or cords.

It is really a matter of putting aside preconceived ideas and being willing to try something new. The canvas threads, even those of rug canvas, are not as tough as they seem, and the firmness of canvas makes it very easy to hold and feed under the machine needle. Nothing much is lost if you break a needle or two at the beginning, but this should not happen if you proceed with caution until you are used to the technique. Of course, the machine may bump a little if the needle pierces a thread rather than passing to one side, but you can avoid this problem by using a ball-point or heavier needle at moderate speed.

With a basic swing-needle machine, you can achieve a variety of effects, and even a straight-stitch machine can fill parts of your canvas with an attractive grainy texture. You can also use automatic stitch patterns on canvas.

Ordinary machine cotton threads can be used for practising, but you will soon want to use machine embroidery cottons, both for their lustrous quality and because the machine seems to work more smoothly with embroidery threads.

Machining with controls at normal

Begin by working lines of close zigzag or satin stitch, guided by the canvas threads. Vary the width of the stitches and the spacing, making wider and narrower stripes and overlapping bands. If you use different colours for the top and bobbin threads, the stitches may have an attractive shadow of the second colour. The important thing is to relax and enjoy this straightforward activity. Later, you can work across the canvas, turning stripes into coloured grids, or experiment with a tacking foot, to produce areas of tufted texture.

Left *This practice piece shows various machine effects: rows of satin stitch of different widths; the back of the stitch worked with too tight a bottom tension; encroaching rows; a grid made by working rows in two directions; and diagonal groups of satin stitches, with the canvas turned 90 degrees after each group.*

Right *Hand stitching on canvas is combined here with machine satin stitch.*

Machining on rug canvas

These eyeglass cases, made by Sue Blake and Audrey King, were produced by machining on canvas.

It is even more satisfying to machine on rug canvas than on finer grades. Again, the canvas is not as impenetrable as it looks. It is, of course, better to position the satin stitches to pass over the threads rather than go through them, but this is no problem.

An exciting new fabric may be created by darning wide fabric strips through the rug canvas grid and machining back and forth to blend the strips together. The canvas almost disappears in this instance, but without its strong support the resulting fabric could not exist. Purses may be made in this way, with satin-stitch seams worked over the cut canvas edges. Choose fabric strips to match other accessories, or work to a theme – for example, April showers, Indian splendour, or lights at night.

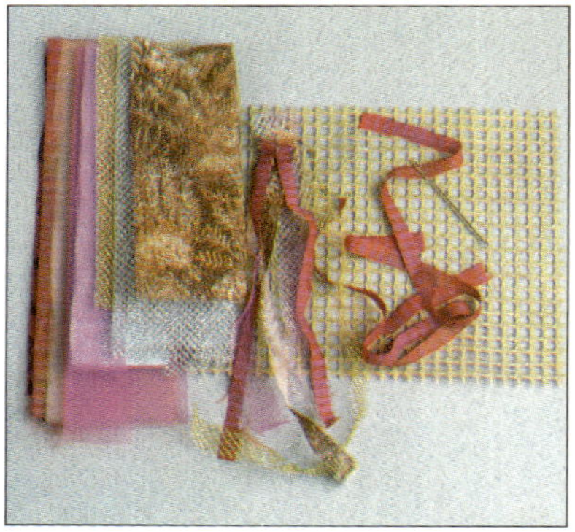

1 **Gather together a selection of fabric strips between 1 and 2cm (½ and ¾in.) wide, including firm cotton strips and lighter nets, glitter and transparent fabrics.**

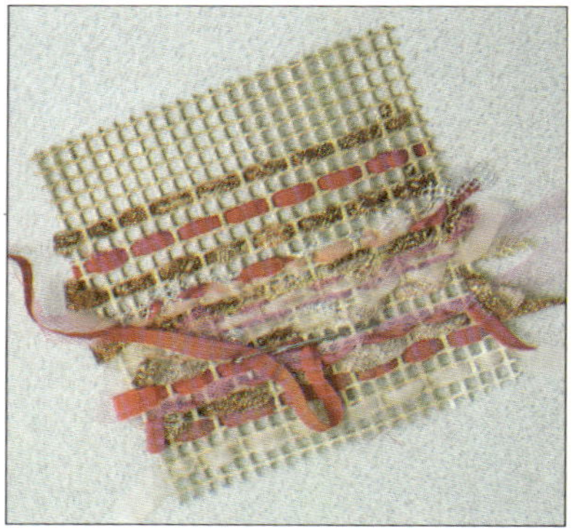

2 **Darn the strips into a coloured canvas, either in stripes or at random. Insert the more solid fabric strips first (any frayed edges will help to blend the final fabric). Add the nets and other fabrics. Leave these darning stitches fairly loose, so that the fabrics bulge or bubble a little above the surface.**

3 **With machine stitch width at 3, and stitch length at 4, machine up and down the darned rows, allowing the machine stitches to blend the fabric strips into a new whole.**

Free machining on canvas

Once you have practised normal machining on canvas, you may choose to expand your skills by experimenting with free machining, which is ideally suited to the flowing patterns of Bargello work and to building up blocks of colour, like satin stitch blocks in hand embroidery. Canvas is an ideal fabric for newcomers to free machining because, unlike most fabrics, it does not need to be held in a frame.

Preparation for free machining varies according to your machine, and details are to be found under darning in most manuals. The feed dogs that move the fabric under the needle must either be lowered or covered, and the presser foot is removed (make sure, however, that the presser foot lever is down before you begin stitching). The stitch length should be 0, and the width may be set as you wish.

These hair ornaments by Jennie Parry were inspired by Indian textile art and were machined on canvases coloured by car spray-paint. One automatic stitch pattern was used throughout. To vary the scale, some rows were stitched to a double size; others were worked on the back of the canvas, using the reverse side of the stitch as part of the pattern. The ornaments are trimmed with beads and rings, hand-made cords and tassels.

1 **Outline a flowing Bargello-type design on the canvas. Turn the canvas so that the sides of the design are at the top and bottom as you work. With the machine prepared for free machine embroidery and with stitch width 4 and length 0, start machining in the central area, moving smoothly forward and from side to side, following the first line of the design.**

2 **When this first line of stitching is completed, fill in the whole area of this colour, overlapping the lines slightly. As each colour is completed, change the thread and move to an adjacent area, working this in the same way.**

Part of a garden border, made with short bursts of satin stitch instead of the smooth forward movement. This builds up blocks of colour, similar to blocks of hand satin stitch.

Lower the needle into the canvas by hand for the first stitch. When you try free machining on canvas, it is important to remember to hold the canvas as flat to the bed of the machine as possible and to move it smoothly under the needle. Work backwards and forwards and from side to side at will, to make continuous lines, changing the colour of the thread as desired.

Darning on canvas

Decorative darning is much more enjoyable than the utilitarian stitches associated with mending, but the process is the same: making lines of running stitches over and under the threads of the fabric. On canvas, this provides a contrast to areas of close formal stitchery, giving a lighter effect, and there may be a subtle shadow of colour where the thread passes along under the canvas. Of course, as some of the canvas threads are visible, making up part of the pattern in certain cases, the canvas will usually need to be coloured.

Darning is worked quite quickly, with one hand on top of an embroidery frame and one below, and it is economical of thread, though the finished piece will not be as hard-wearing as formally stitched pieces.

You may use darning stitches freely (1, 2) to fill in an area, to put a skimming of colour across unworked canvas, in a sky for example, or to build up large-scale formal patterns. The stitches may be of uniform or random lengths and rows may be horizontal, vertical, diagonal, or combinations of these. It is most common to finish each row before beginning the next and to work each row in one direction only, but of course there is room to experiment. You may use any size of canvas and any thread or group of threads. If the latter are so thick that they distort the canvas, a new design possibility is opened up.

Pattern darning (3, 4) involves a more formal arrangement of running stitches. Stitches of set lengths build up into regular patterns, these can either be used to fill in shapes or the entire design may be formed with strong bands of pattern darning. The final effect is rather like weaving, with a reverse image on the back.

1 Free diagonal darning with threads and fabric strips may be used as a fabric in its own right or as a background to intensely stitched areas.

2 Small areas of horizontal darning, made with a textured thread, are combined with lines of diagonal darning. Only three space-dyed threads have been used.

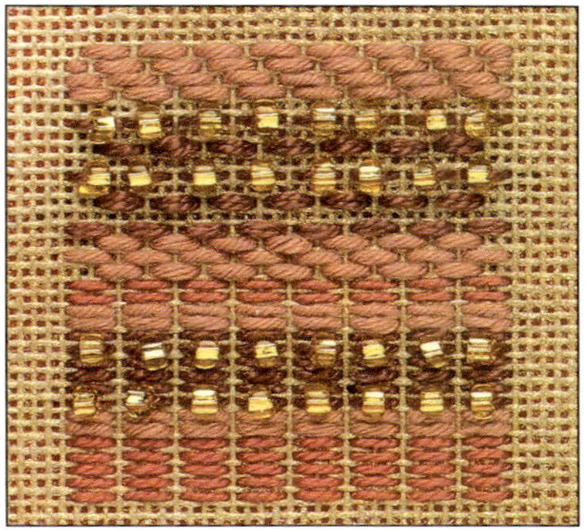

3 The regular darning seen here is counted over three threads and under one. It is stitched in various arrangements, including bricking and stepping, and beads have been added.

4 Shapes filled with fine pattern darning may be used to provide a light contrast to heavily stitched areas.

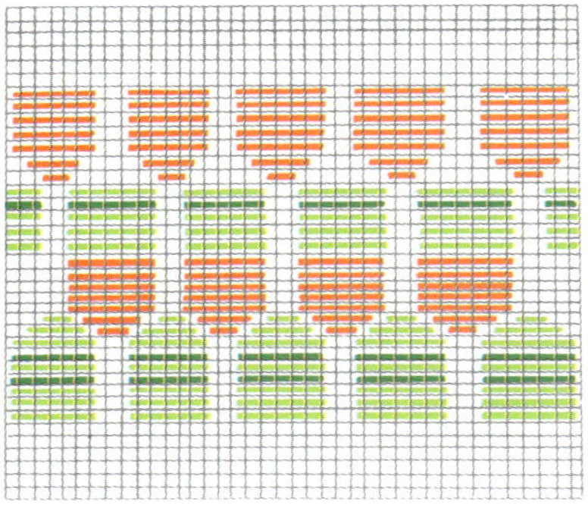

5 Complex darning patterns should be worked out on graph paper (keep a needle and some canvas close by to check if the pattern is viable). Instead of colouring in the squares, in which case each square would represent one canvas thread, it is clearer and simpler to use the printed lines to represent the canvas threads, and to draw in the darning stitches as lines crossing the grid. Remember to follow through each line of stitching in one colour.

Combining different canvases

Variety of scale has traditionally been given to canvaswork embroidery by using fine and coarse canvases in the same piece; a fine detailed insert may be grafted into a coarser main ground, or a landscape, for example, may be worked on three grades of canvas, a coarse-mesh canvas being used for the large-scale foreground, medium for the middle ground, and fine for the distance. The method used to combine these canvases will depend on the purpose of the embroidery – whether, as a useful article, it will be handled a great deal, or whether it will be purely decorative – and on the nature of the canvas used.

Interlock canvas will not easily fray and may be trimmed close, to overlap or underlie the cut-away areas of the main canvas. Stitches can then be worked over the join in a straightforward way. On the other hand, interlock canvas is unsuitable for the traditional grafting-in method shown here, as it will not fray or unravel. The threads of canvases that have been dyed with car spray will also be too stiff for this method.

If you are embroidering a formal piece that involves joining different grades of canvas, you should experiment before you begin in order to decide whether to attempt an invisible grafted join, whether to hide the join beneath compatible stitches, or whether to make a feature of the join by emphasizing it with strong edge stitches, couched threads or cords. In formal work, these decisions should really be made at the design stage – it is heart-breaking to stitch most of the embroidery only to find that the pieces do not join well. However, a completely different and original piece of embroidery may evolve when things have not gone as planned, and a feeling of 'Nothing ventured, nothing gained' prevails.

Grafting-in (1, 2, 3, 4)

This is suitable for formal work and results in a firm durable join, though it is a rather intricate and time-consuming technique. The basic method can also be adapted to apply worked canvas embroidery to fabrics (preferably thick ones, such as tweed or fine woollens) that are not evenweave.

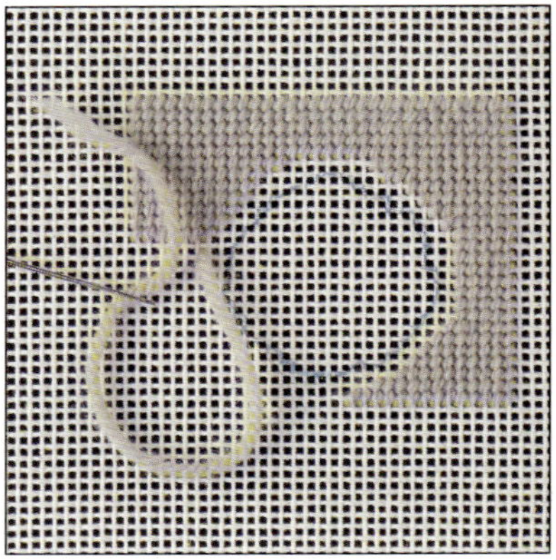

1 **On the coarser canvas, mark the position for the piece to be inserted and stitch the background embroidery almost to this outline.**

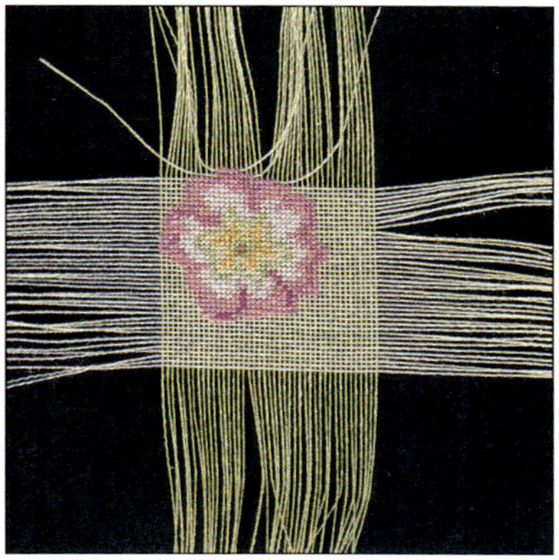

2 Stitch the fine embroidery in the centre of a piece of fine canvas, leaving a minimum of 5cm (2in.) unworked all round. A larger margin – up to 8cm (3in.) – will make the task much easier, though it is wasteful of canvas. Gently fray out the canvas right up to the embroidery.

3 Baste the fine motif in position on the coarse canvas. Thread a needle with single or pairs of the frayed-out threads; draw them through to the back, and darn them into the coarse canvas.

4 When all the threads have been taken through, complete the background stitching right up to the inserted piece.

Overlapping and underlaying

When joining pieces of canvas into decorative panels that will not be much handled, there is great scope for individual ingenuity. Remember, however, that the finished embroidery will be difficult, if not impossible, to stretch. It is better to work with such pieces fixed to a plain wood frame with drawing pins (thumb tacks), as a taut tension is not desirable during the joining process.

Pieces of embroidered canvas may be sewn on top of canvas of a different scale, the edges being concealed under stitching. They need

In Sweet Peas, *Peggy Field used two grades of canvas in order to make some of the plants appear to grow behind others. The joins of the overlapped canvas, first secured by herringbone stitch, are hidden partly by the canvas stitches and partly by the cords stitched on top.*

not be applied flat, but may be padded or manipulated, perhaps by folding or pleating, before being attached.

Holes may be cut out from the main piece of canvas, and other canvas attached beneath. Care should be taken that the top canvas is not weakened, and that it is not distorted by a tight tension. Non-fray interlock canvas is best, but touches of glue on the underside of the mesh of loosely woven canvas will help to strengthen it. Use a toothpick or match stick to apply the glue, as a light hand is essential. When the glue is dry, baste the insert in place with small stitches in a matching thread. Hand or machine stitches may be worked over the edges, the embroidery being removed from the frame (if one is used) for the machining.

Beryl Taylor used three different sizes of canvas to make In the Greenhouse*: the large-scale leaf stitching contrasts with the finer flower areas, and the finest canvas is used for the distant view. The formal and free stitches use a variety of threads and fabric strips.*

Mineral, *by Beryl Court, is a complex panel, inspired by a piece of mineral. Three grades of canvas, stitched by hand and machine, have been integrated by further machine stitchery, applied cords and fabric strips into an original piece with subtle textural interest.*

Tramming, couching and laid work

Tramming is an age-old technique in which the design is indicated by long basting or darning stitches in wools of appropriate colours. Traditionally, these stitches were laid between the narrow pairs of threads of Penelope (double) canvas. Besides marking out the design, the tramming gave a padded effect to thinner stitches that were worked into the larger holes. Tramming also made the finished article more hard-wearing.

Established practices of this type may often be either discarded or radically adapted to produce work that is different and exciting. Take time to think about a procedure and the possible departures from it: even if a finished experimental embroidery is not completely satisfying, it is the thought and exploration that has gone into its making that matters, and you will probably be able to draw on this experience at a later date. Your experiments may lead you into an entirely different kind of embroidery, but the exact classification is of no real importance as long as the piece is effective.

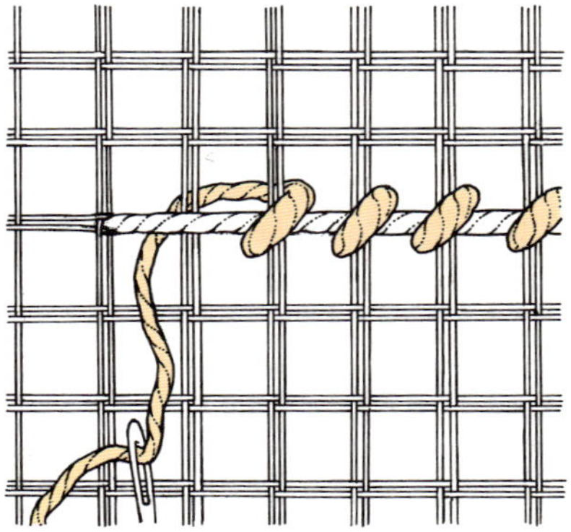

1 Traditional tramming features tent stitch over a matching tramming thread laid between the pairs of threads of double canvas.

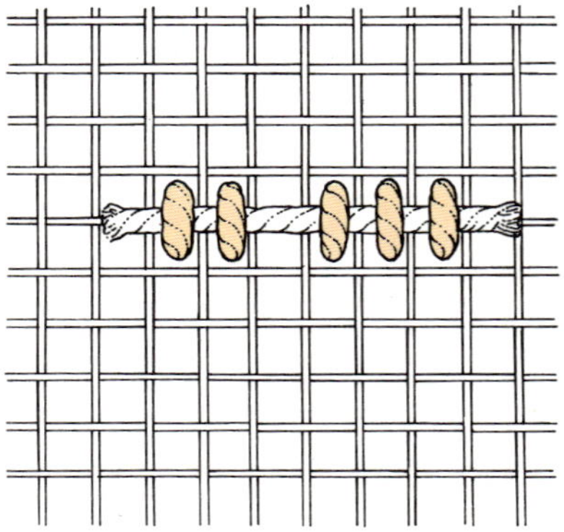

2 In this diagram of experimental tramming, spaced Gobelin stitch in a contrast colour is worked over a tramming thread laid on top of one thread of single canvas.

The canvas

You may choose to colour the canvas so that unworked areas match or contrast with the tramming or stitching. If you use single instead of double canvas, you can choose where to lay the tramming: you may lay the tramming thread along a canvas thread and stitch into the holes at each side, or you may stitch or lay it between two canvas threads. In this case you may either make large stitches over the two threads and tramming or bring small stitches up through the hole, over the tramming, and back down through the same hole.

The tramming thread

You may experiment with the tramming thread, using its colour to contrast and interplay with the embroidery stitches. You may choose metallic or shiny tramming threads, or depart from the normal scale by using thick textured wools, ribbons or fabric strips. You might even tram with long bugle beads, coloured straws or perspex rods.

If the tramming is no longer functional, you can play with the spacing, using it in alternate rows or parts of a row. Vertical or

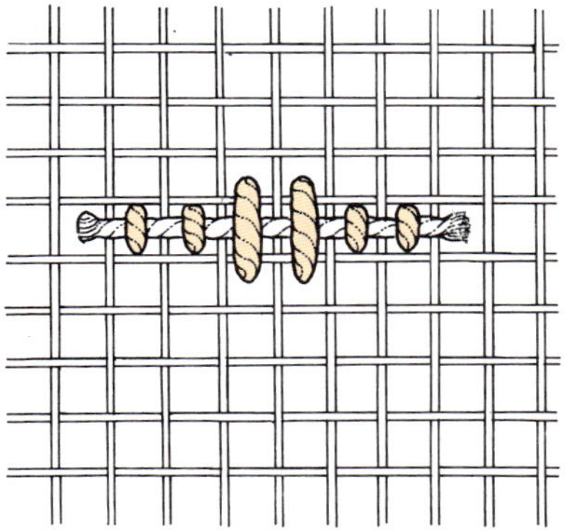

3 **Another departure from convention shows two sizes of Gobelin stitch in a contrast colour worked over a tramming thread laid between two threads of single canvas.**

4 **In this sample, buttonhole stitch is worked over a vertical tramming of fabric strips. The roses are freely couched.**

5 **Here, half cross stitch has been worked on a vertical and horizontal tramming of fabric strips.**

In Flowers in the Grass, *by Patricia Batts, the tramming of torn strips of hand-dyed silk, ribbons and thick threads is held down by minimal embroidery stitches. The canvas holds the torn strips firm: the work could not exist without its canvas base.*

Part of a sampler, dated 1913, shows canvas stitched with metal threads and patterning similar to or nué.

diagonal tramming may result in very free work.

Of course, when the tramming thread is emphasized, you are moving towards couching and laid work, and if you use metallic threads you may produce a coarse form of *or nué*, the shaded gold of ecclesiastical embroidery. However, the use of canvas makes such work easier and opens up areas for experimental work.

The embroidery stitches

The third area to think about is that of the embroidery, or holding down, stitches. Conventional tramming is used most often with tent, half cross and Gobelin stitches, but spaced cross stitches, fern stitch, diagonal stitch and numerous other stitches may also be used. Once again, you can change their colour and experiment with the spacing – regularly, randomly, or to a set pattern. And, of course, the threads can be sewn down by machine.

In this section of a sampler by Jennie Parry, there are many variations of battlement couching, with threads laid and couched vertically and horizontally. This piece emerged from research into the filling stitches of crewel work, canvas being a much easier fabric on which to work than the traditional linen twill.

In Butterfly Wings, *June Linsley uses a horizontal tramming of space-dyed threads, patterned with Gobelin stitches in the manner of* or nué. *The iridescent thread suggests the quality of the wing scales, and the unravelled threads represent the tiny hairs on the magnified wing.*

Canvas with appliqué

An effective contrast to stitched canvas may be provided by smoother areas of applied fabric, suede or leather, either sewn down flat, or perhaps slightly padded. Smooth leather or suede pieces, for example, might be applied as paving stones to contrast with vegetation worked in highly textured stitches, or a slightly padded monogram could be raised from a stitched background as part of a personalized article.

The cut-out shapes are sewn to the canvas, either before the embroidery is begun or part-way through, so that the stitching can be worked right up to the edges of these applied pieces.

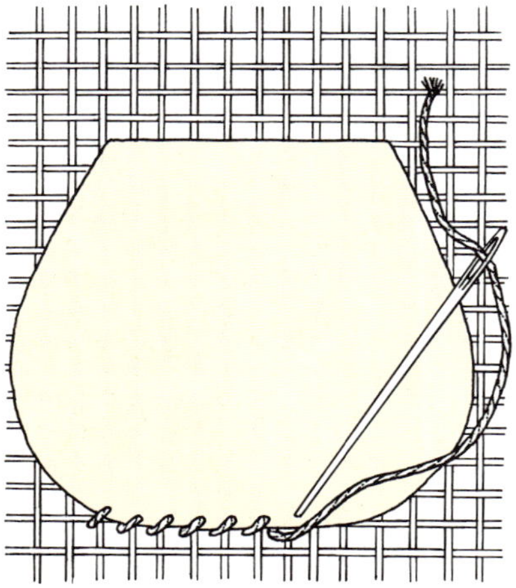

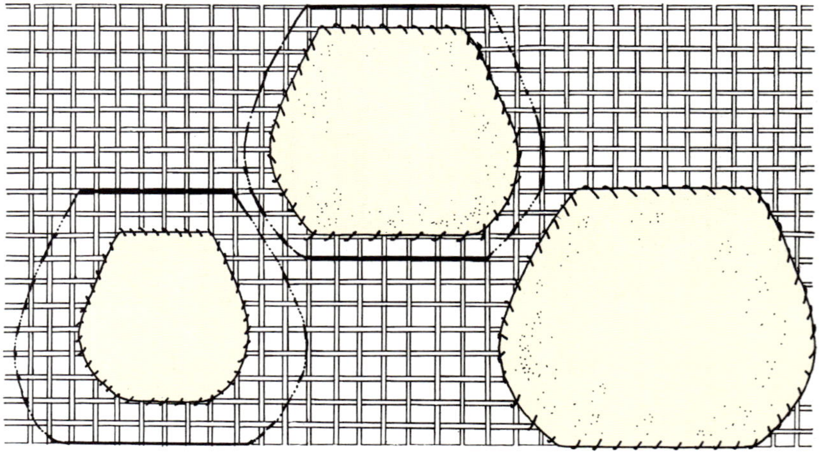

1 **To apply flat leather or felt shapes to canvas, use a sharp sewing needle and matching thread. Bring the needle up through the canvas and down through the applied shape: this will make it easier to ensure that stitches are evenly spaced. To add a little padding to a simple outline, ease shredded polyester batting or wadding underneath the shape when the stitching is almost complete.**

2 **For a smoothly padded contour and more complicated shapes, use layers of felt to build up a filling under the top fabric. First cut out the appliqué shape, adding a seam allowance all around if you are applying a frayable fabric that needs to be turned under. Cut out a felt shape, slightly smaller than the finished size of the appliqué shape. Cut two or three more felt shapes – as many as are required to raise the shape sufficiently – cutting each successively smaller than the one before. Draw the outline of the appliqué on the canvas and stitch the smallest felt shape in the centre of the outline. Over it, stitch the second shape, and so on, finishing with the top fabric.**

In this detail from Hydrangeas, *by Phyllis Gunstone, the shapes of applied leather have been built up with layers of felt.*

To recreate the textures of autumn underfoot, Jackey Hill used small slivers of suede and leather, partially attached to the background of bullion knots, velvet stitch and fine tent stitch.

For a more textured effect, use slivers of thick fabric or leather, attaching them at one end only, and leaving the other end free. Ribbons, fabric strips and cords that you have made yourself can also be applied to canvas, either as straight lines in a background, or in formal or random curving patterns.

Collage appliqué

A different way of using applied fabric on canvas is to choose pieces of finer materials, tacking them to the canvas as a kind of collage background for your stitches. The fabric may echo the shape of fairly formal stitches: square fabric pieces, for example, might form a background to variations of cushion stitch. In this case, you should choose a transparent fabric, so that you can still see the grid of the canvas as you stitch, and you will require a needle with a sharp point.

Alternatively, thicker fabric pieces may play a more dominant part on the canvas, providing a strong fabric emphasis against the stitched background. Baste the fabric pieces in position, then work up to and even over them with your stitches.

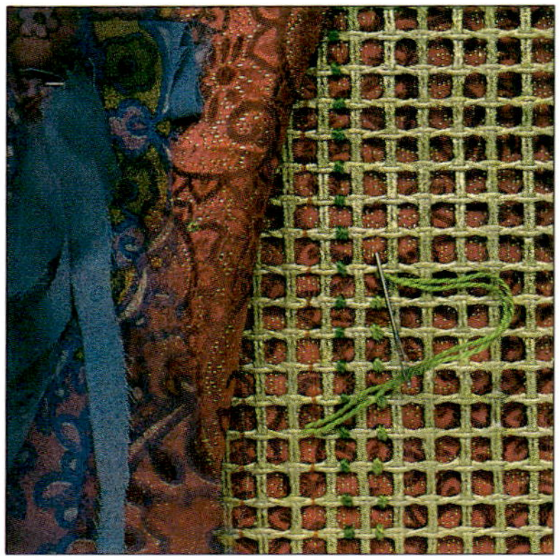

1 To create a new fabric, Sheila Gray bastes a piece of brocade to the back of rug canvas that has been sprayed gold. A frame is not necessary for a small area, but it is easier to use one for larger pieces. (Some basting stitches are here shown in green, for clarity, but in actual work the threads should be as unobtrusive as possible.)

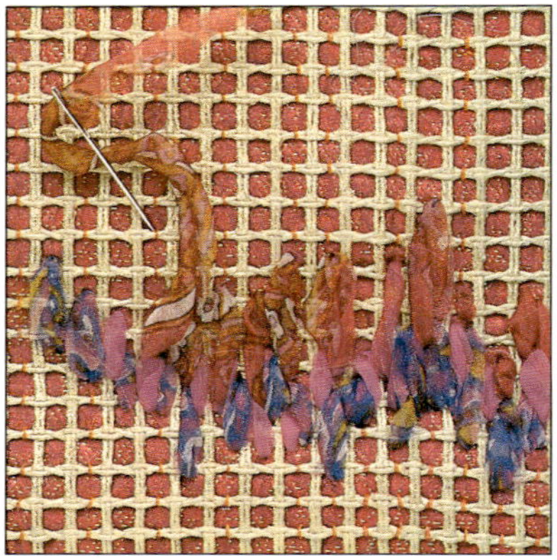

2 Free Bargello stitchery is worked through the two layers, using fabric strips in scale with the coarse mesh. A chenille needle with a sharp point is needed.

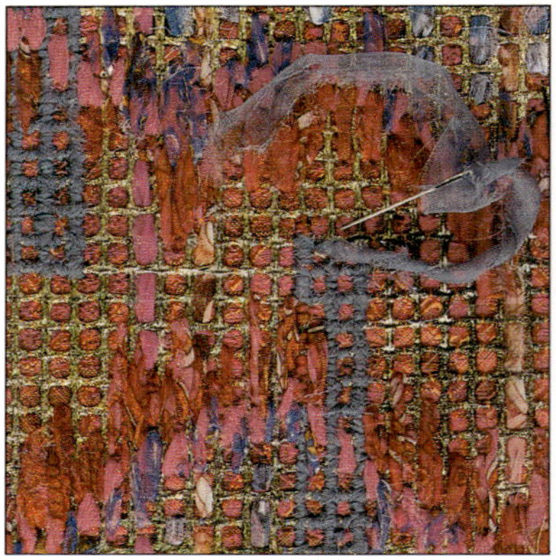

3 Lines of darning stitch are added, and small straight stitches are worked around the square mesh of the rug canvas in certain areas. The brocade showing through the unworked parts of the canvas plays an important part in the final effect.

In a collage appliqué sample by Evelyn Luxford, free straight stitches are worked as a background and at the same time attach random fabric shapes made by bonding.

Sandwich appliqué

Original combinations of fabric and canvas may be produced by backing a relatively coarse coloured canvas with a piece of fabric, before working stitches over only part of the area. You can even sandwich several layers of canvas and fabric together and stitch through the sandwich by hand or machine. The stitches can either be very strong or quite minimal, serving merely to hold the layers together. You could then cut away parts of the top layers to create even greater contrast.

Fabrics not usually associated with canvas may be used, such as rich brocade, patterned chiffons or bonded fabrics of your own creation, incorporating fragments of net, lurex and lace. The very rich effects obtained in this way may exist in their own right as abstract decorative panels, or be used as new fabrics for cushions, purses or bags.

Squares of semi-transparent fabric were basted to canvas as a background to formal stitching – variations of cushion stitch – in this collage appliqué sample by June Linsley.

Coloured rug canvas has been laid by Barbara Furse over fabric of stained glass colours. A narrow zigzag machine stitch has been worked over a grid trimmed to stepped shapes. The rows are mounted at different levels.

Canvas embroidery with needleweaving

Needleweaving is a drawn-thread technique in which the horizontal threads of the fabric are withdrawn and the embroidery threads are woven into or wrapped around the remaining vertical fabric threads, either freely or in a pattern. Ribbons or laces may also be threaded through the weaving, or a woven piece may be mounted on a complementary fabric.

Needleweaving can be combined successfully with canvas stitches, giving variety to a design. The area to be worked in needleweaving should be prepared first by removing the horizontal threads before the canvas is put on a frame. The canvas embroidery stitches should then be worked before the needleweaving, otherwise the canvas may warp. After this, the needleweaving should be

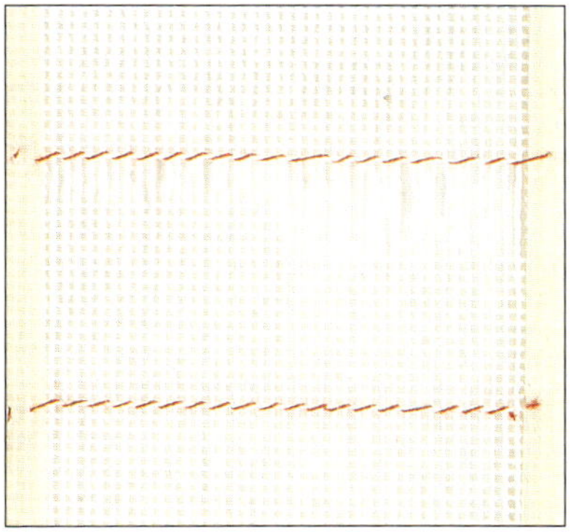

1 **Decide upon the area of needleweaving. Oversew along the border of the threads that are to be withdrawn in order to keep the remaining threads in place. Snip the threads to be withdrawn up the centre of the area, taking care not to damage the vertical threads. Remove the snipped threads using your tapestry needle.**

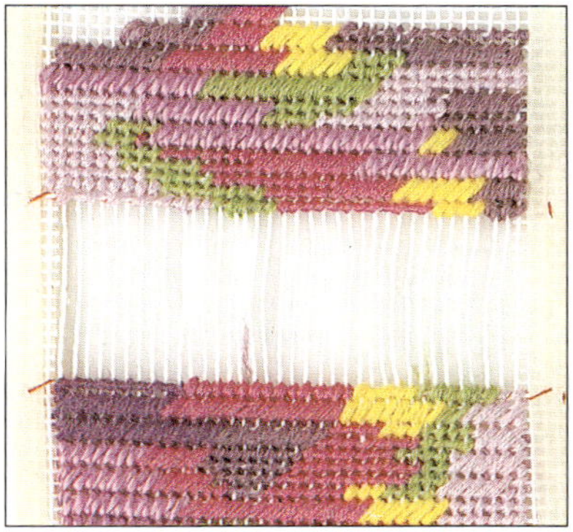

2 **Work the canvas stitches right up to the open threads, hiding the oversewing.**

3 **Anchor your weaving thread under the canvas stitches and weave in and out of the vertical threads. Sometimes weave a figure-of-eight around two threads and sometimes take in more. Leave the thread hanging at the end of a colour block, until there is a woven bar through which it can be taken to the point where it will next be needed. Alternatively, finish it off behind the canvas stitches.**

started at the top, the thread being anchored underneath the already worked canvas stitches. Try to avoid joining on thread in the middle of the weaving. To finish off the thread, take it to the wrong side of the work and anchor it at the back of the canvas stitches again.

Although the piece illustrated has bands of needleweaving running across the work, this is not necessarily the only possibility: you might try surrounding small areas of needleweaving with canvas stitches. In this case, the horizontal threads should be withdrawn to each side of an area intended for needleweaving. They should then be left until the canvas stitches have been finished, after which the loose threads of canvas should be woven into the back of the embroidered areas before you begin to work a pattern of needleweaving on the vertical threads.

A tissue paper collage of a potted chrysanthemum plant, showing the area chosen to be worked.

A panel worked by Peggy Field from her collage: the top part is worked in tent stitch, and the pattern is carried through to the rows of needleweaving and the row of beading, finishing with Gobelin stitches. The beads are sewn directly onto the bare canvas.

Canvas and pulled work

If you pull your needlepoint stitches too tightly, the canvas threads will be drawn together, but what may appear to be a minor disaster can take you to another technique.

In pulled or drawn fabric work, the threads of a loose evenweave material are drawn together by very tight stitches to create patterns of holes – a type of geometric openwork. Matching thread is used, as the stitches are less important than the holes that they make by distorting the spacing of the threads. Provided you use a woven canvas, not the interlock variety, this technique converts very readily to canvas, and you will find that you already know the main stitches that may be used – eyelets, back stitch, and the straight stitches called upright Gobelin and cushion stitch. You may use any grade of woven canvas, as coarse as 10 threads to the inch if you wish.

These simple examples of pulled work were made on two scales of canvas, 10 and 20 holes to the inch. Matching threads were used in the traditional way to create patterns of holes.

Experiments towards a piece on tropical butterflies, by Joyce Kohn, feature pulled Gobelin stitches, tent stitch and darning, on canvas coloured with drawing ink. Silk and metallic threads are used.

Black work

A visit to a museum can often provide ideas for creative experiments. In their canvaswork the Victorians sometimes included areas of canvas lace: using only their favourite cross stitch, the more solid areas of the pattern were stitched in thick black silk or wool, while fine black silk created the effect of open net in others – a simple kind of black work in fact.

This idea can be adopted today for cross stitch designs, using two thicknesses of thread on fine canvas, natural or coloured. The resulting embroidery may have a light delicate effect or a rich heavy quality, depending on the materials chosen.

Care must be taken in fastening on and off when stitching, or irrelevant threads or stitches on the back of the work may create shadows on the front. On the other hand, perhaps this might offer the opportunity to experiment with a different kind of shadow work, with the pattern showing through a canvas grid.

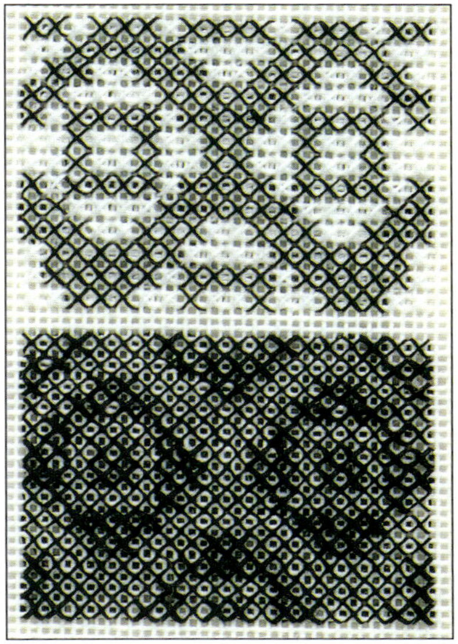

Experiments by Joan Hake show the effects created by different weights of thread and sizes of stitch.

This cross stitch design is worked with wool and sewing thread to give the effect of Victorian canvas lace. The pattern is worked first with wool and the background is filled in afterwards.

Using rug canvas

Rug canvas, with its large square mesh, is becoming very popular with embroiderers, not necessarily for embroidered rugs and carpets, as in the past, but as a versatile medium for use in many different ways.

Obviously, it offers a suitable scale for a major piece of work, designed for spacious surroundings, and the large stitches that are possible on such canvas can make strong marks, with a dramatic impact not otherwise easily achieved. Rug canvas may also be used for other traditional techniques based on a square grid, and it is useful as a presentation material. It can even be used as a stencil if you need to transfer a grid pattern to a background for other types of embroidery.

Designs

If your natural tendency is to work small, a change to a larger scale, if only for one piece, may have a liberating and beneficial effect. You will be obliged to re-evaluate the scale of your designs, the stitches that you choose and the materials with which you work. It is interesting and fun to try to work out the same subject on both a small and large scale, but the results will be more successful if you plan a large-scale design in its own terms. If your inspiration is a transparency, a slide projector may help you to decide the most effective size.

A full-scale collage with paper scraps from colour magazines is a helpful next step, the variations of colour printing suggesting ways of handling the large masses of colour involved in this kind of work.

Stitches and threads

Large bold stitches will obviously make strong marks, viewed both near and at a distance. In general, simple stitches seem to work most effectively: cross stitch, for example, as in 'Sweet Williams', or the upright Gobelin used for 'Haystacks'. Back stitch worked on the front of the canvas looks very different to back stitch worked on the reverse side. Half cross stitch, worked with a thinner thread than the canvas would usually dictate, looks like wrapping. French knots

For Sweet Williams, *Sue Armstrong used two sizes of cross stitch for the background of flowers and foliage, which she worked in a range of mat and shiny threads, thick wools, raffene, fabric strips and ribbons. Loops of silk form the flowers in the foreground, giving them a three-dimensional effect.*

and loop stitches will give texture, and simplified eyelets, worked over one thread of the canvas only, may build up into softer areas, according to the thread used.

Rug wool, which might seem the obvious choice for working on rug canvas, is best avoided as those qualities that make it suitable for hard wear underfoot give a flat, heavy look to purely decorative work. There are great creative possibilities in the use of the thicker knitting yarns: mohair, for example, can give an unusual misty effect to background areas. Fabric strips – both cut and torn – can prove very useful. Cut edges make a bold impact, whereas the frayed edges of torn strips may soften the impact of a strong stitch, giving it added interest at close quarters. Silk, chiffon and net strips can create areas of great delicacy within the stronger image.

If the thread used for stitching covers the canvas thread but does not completely fill the hole, the resulting effect looks rather like openwork embroidery. Such areas may be backed with fabric of contrasting colour or sheen to add yet another dimension, or the holes may be left as holes.

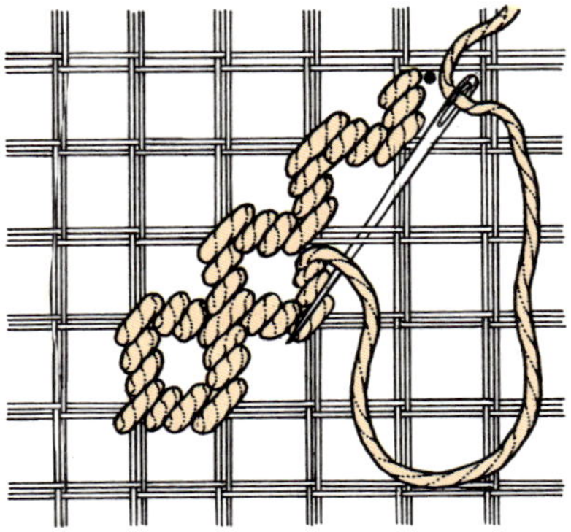

1 **Two rows of diagonal overcasting build up into small squares.**

2 **In this diagram of simple lacis darning, the darning stitches are worked over and under the threads of rug canvas.**

In Pink Metallic, *by Pat Iles, the small units were made by layering various mesh fabrics, dyed lace and net curtaining, and combining them with free machine stitching. They were then attached to a full square of rug canvas, parts of which were cut away to leave a unifying structure.*

Rug canvas for other techniques

If you make a feature of the holes, you are near to achieving, though with a different scale and texture, some of the effects of drawn-thread work of the Hardanger variety, in which groups of both vertical and horizontal threads are removed, creating a mesh of holes. Rug canvas, of course, provides a ready-made mesh on which you may enjoy experimenting, saving yourself the time and trouble of creating a drawn-thread network.

Fillet darning or lacis work is another traditional technique which makes use of a square mesh. In the past, the mesh was hand-knotted and threads were darned or woven to fill in parts of the mesh. The resulting geometric designs produced a rather chunky kind of square lace. The panel 'No traycloths at Greenham Common' makes use of this late Victorian technique to emphasize the connection between the Suffragettes and modern women protesting against nuclear arms bases.

Rug canvas as a presentation medium

In modern embroideries, rug canvas is often used as a background for mounting a number of smaller pieces. These may be purely experimental fragments, with a common shape or theme, or more closely and intentionally related pieces of canvas or other embroidery. The rug canvas mesh – dyed, sprayed or overcast in related colourways – can hold small pieces together, both literally and metaphorically, uniting them in an integrated whole.

The above interpretations all take advantage of the geometric nature of the canvas grid to a lesser or greater extent, incorporating canvas and counted thread stitches. It is possible, of course, to use the canvas for entirely free work. In larger panels, the firmness of the canvas gives a support that is lacking with finer fabrics, however taut they may be in the frame. Almost any surface embroidery stitches may be adapted to this type of canvas, provided you select threads of a compatible scale.

Rug canvas is ideal for large-scale embroideries. Tulips and Wallflowers *was Patricia Elkington's first embroidery on this scale, and the rug canvas provided a firm grid to support the free stitchery – layers of darning, fly stitch and Italian buttonhole insertion stitch. Some of the tulips are applied shapes of darned sequin waste; others are fine canvas, with Gobelin filling stitch.*

A large-scale work – Haystacks *– by Elizabeth Ashurst is here seen at various stages – a selection of preparatory materials, and the finished piece. (Photograph of corn by Bill Mason.)*

Rug canvas was chosen for the finished panel (photograph by Keith Harding) because it offered a suitable scale for the subject. The use of two sizes of canvas gives a feeling of distance. Strips of hand-dyed silk and ribbons were used for upright Gobelin stitches of the foreground area, which are combined with overlayers of slanting stitches made with wools and perlé threads.

The mark made by a stitch – its impact and degree of intensity – will be different on different types of canvas. Julia Caprara chooses her stitches and her fabric with deliberation.

The theme of Colour Sound – Coming together – Water with Fire *is the idea of the unifying of opposites – natural and artificial, warm and cold, concentrated and diffused.*

This theme is echoed by the choice of materials. At the heart of the panel, a variety of natural and manmade materials are held together by small tight cross stitches on a relatively fine mesh. This close image gradually diffuses into larger, looser and more random stitching on the coarse grid of the rug canvas. The latter remains, almost invisible but still present, under the smoother outer areas of applied silk and dyed tissue paper.

Embroidering events and ideas

Among the most interesting pieces of embroidery that have survived from the past are those that commemorate or refer to a dated event – public or private. These sometimes allow us a glimpse either of the person who embroidered the piece or of life at that time. The simplest modern sampler welcoming a new arrival in the family will be treasured by its owner in later years, and embroideries commenting on the current social or political scene are growing in number.

Once you start thinking along these lines, you will discover that canvas embroidery is an exciting and unusual medium for expressing ideas. Whatever shade of political opinion appeals to you, you will enjoy creating an embroidery all the more if it is a personal statement of your view of events and ideas. After all, when you consider how much time and effort is put into a finished piece, it is only fair that it should express something of your individuality, character and beliefs, and even though the heat may die out of the current political issue, and future generations may not fully understand what you were saying, they will still be interested and intrigued. (Incidentally, it is important, in this context, always to sign and date your work.)

'No Traycloths at Greenham Common' celebrates the spirit of two groups of non-conforming women who endured great hardship in the pursuit of their ideals. Rug canvas is used as a background for ease of construction of this larger piece, but more importantly, its grid is used as symbolic of their repression.

The connection is made between the Suffragettes who were reviled in their own time, but who are now revered for their struggle to obtain votes for women in the early years of this century, and the women who protested about nuclear bases at Greenham Common, in England, and who were similarly reviled and mocked in the mid-1980s. The Suffragettes broke through the repressive grid of conventional behaviour, abandoning their ladylike pursuits, symbolized by white work embroidery (whose upkeep and laundering oppressed yet another class of women). The modern campaigners against nuclear weapons also broke away from accepted behaviour to besiege the physical grid of the wire and netting defending the nuclear bases.

Great Britain, 1987, *by June Linsley, includes tent stitch with three-dimensional figures on a collage background.*

GREAT BRITAIN

Colour adds to the meaning of the piece, the white giving way to the green and purple of the Suffragette colours, and then moving into the rainbow colours that symbolize peace.

'Great Britain 1987' was begun when the result of the elections seemed to promise further divisions between the 'haves' and 'have nots'. The phrases 'fat cats', 'sweeping the rubbish under the carpet' and 'a threadbare society' were in the embroiderer's mind. The idea that it would be desirable to return to Victorian values was current at the time, and as she began to stitch the fat cat on the mat she remembered the Victorian love of embroidering their pampered pets sitting on cushions – the work began to accumulate additional layers of meaning.

The 'rules' of canvas work were purposely ignored. A diagonal distortion was allowed to develop, and wool that would not cover the canvas was chosen to leave threadbare and faded areas as secondary references to the state of the nation. Finally, a collage of newspaper cuttings was added as background to the grotesque 'forgotten' figures.

In No Traycloths at Greenham Common, *June Linsley combined lacis work, cords and tassels on a background of sprayed figures, to make a large-scale embroidery.*

INDEX

ACKNOWLEDGMENTS

We should like to thank all those who lent us their work for this book, in particular our own students and the embroidery students of Windsor and Maidenhead College of Further Education and their tutors.

We are grateful to Beryl and Dudley Tucker for their help with frames and to the Bogod Machine Co. Ltd, Distributors of Bernina Sewing Machines, for the loan of a machine. Mulberry Silks of Chipping Norton were most generous in supplying silk threads, samples of canvas were kindly provided by the Chipping Campden Needlework Centre and Mace and Nairn of Salisbury, and Needle Art International of Chelmsford supplied us with plastic canvas.

Peggy Field
June Linsley